Beyond the First 48

Shawn Wright

Beyond the First 48
Copyright © 2024 by Shawn Wright

All rights reserved. Printed in the United States of America. No part of this book may be used or reproduced in any manner whatsoever without written permission except in the case of brief quotations embodied in critical articles and reviews. Permission granted on request.

Qui 2 Life Publishing
34 Shining Willow Way
LaPlata, MD 20646
www.qui2life.com
1 (301) 710-5219

Print ISBN: 979-8-9869513-6-2

eBook ISBN: 979-8-9869513-7-9

Library of Congress Cataloging-in-Publication

Author Name: Shawn Wright

Title: Beyond the First 48

Edited by: Tania Easterling and T. Lynn Tate

Cover Design by: Olayemi Bolaji

Qui 2 Life Publishing is not responsible for any content or determination of work. All information is solely considered as the point of view of the author.

This book is dedicated to all of the families whose lives have been impacted by gun violence. Although our outcomes may vary, You are not alone.

Acknowledgments

First and foremost, I want to thank God. Without him, this book wouldn't be possible.

I want to thank my publisher, T. Lynn Tate, for taking on this project and helping me get my story out there. I appreciate and love her for doing that.

When I told my children, Avery, Brianna, and Chris, I wanted to write a book about our experience; all three were supportive and encouraged me. Thank you, and I love you guys with all my heart.

Thank you to all of Chris' friends who came to the hospital and those who couldn't but sent me and his siblings a message of encouragement. A special thank you goes to Darius, Chris' best friend. Forever brothers, you all have an unbreakable bond. We love and appreciate you.

To my mother, Gladys, twin sister, Dawn, and brother, Brucie, you all were my rock through the whole ordeal. I love you guys for everything. Thank you, Kimaada (my childhood friend), for praying and checking on us through this experience. Also, my stepbrothers and sisters - Linda, Andre, Shalene, Shonia, Antwan, Willie Jr., and Jamison- thank you for always making your sis laugh when I needed it. Love you guys.

A huge thank you to Chris' father, Shawn, and the Vanderhorst family. Shawn, you asked questions I couldn't and ensured we were well informed during our son's crisis. Thank you to Glennis, Tee, Jamal, and Ruthanne for giving me strength and support when I needed it the most. You all showed so much love for not only Chris but me as well. To the rest of the Vanderhorst family who couldn't be at the hospital but made sure we knew that we were in your thoughts and prayers, we love and thank you, too.

Thank you, Money! You and your family were very supportive during our time of need and are still a part of our lives. Money, I know this experience affected you as much as it affected me, and your strength and support helped me and the children during this ordeal. The love you have for my children goes beyond words, and for that, I say thank you.

My aunts and uncles – Frances, JB, Jackie, Gregory, Lynn, Debbie, and my great Aunt Audrey for calling and coming to the hospital, lending support and prayer over me, Chris, Avery, and Brianna. We appreciate and love you. My Aunt Doris and my Wright family, thank you for calling and checking on Chris and me. To Chris (Chris' namesake), thank you for always checking on me no matter what. We will get justice for your son, Andre. I love you more than you know, cousin.

My high school friends – Elanda, Deborah, Virginia, Kena, Stephanie, and Susan – you all were with me during my darkest hour. You prayed for me and made me laugh when I needed it the most. You guys are the greatest, and I love you always.

Thank you to my Georgetown Campus Colleagues. After finding out what happened to Chris, you all lent a listening ear and heart. I am forever grateful and love you guys.

To my friend and former colleague, Tara Hill-Starks, you often listened to me talk about our experience and told me I needed to write a book. I am so glad you encouraged me to write this book. With all my heart, I thank you, Tara!

A special thank you to my friends, Vincent and Cathy Myers, who stopped by the hospital to pray for us. You guys have a special place in my heart always.

Thank you to the numerous people from all over who prayed for me and my family and offered support and encouragement during our experience. My family and I can't thank you enough for being there for us. We will always be grateful for your support.

Above all, thank you, readers. I hope I have helped and encouraged anyone who has gone through a traumatic experience to know you are not alone. Together, we are showing a personal side to gun violence and its effects on family, friends, and the community. I pray one day, we will end gun violence. Until then, we continue to fight.

Introduction

The song "Smile," written by John Turner and Geoffrey Parsons, comes to mind whenever I feel overwhelmed. I remember hearing this song for the first time during Michael Jackson's funeral when his older brother Jermaine sang it. During his eulogy for his brother, Jermaine mentioned it was Michael's favorite song.

As I listened to the lyrics, I felt so connected to this song. Although the words seemed sad and lonely, I truly understood what the songwriters meant. They were encouraging us to smile through the pain and sorrow we experience, as it is temporary.

The songwriters wrote, *"Smile, though your heart is aching. Smile, even though it's breaking."*

Honestly, it felt like he had taken the pages of my life and turned them into a song.

My smile is the essence of who I am and how I often navigate life. Through the hardships, milestones, and triumphs, **I smile!** No one knows my pain. No one knows my sorrow. No one knows but me. I smile through life, even during trying times as an African-American woman and single mother, and believe me, it is not easy.

Introduction

When a woman is about to become a mother, it is the most exciting time of her life because she is bringing new life into the world. She thinks of all the things she wants to teach her child. She thinks about how the things she learned throughout her life may benefit in raising her child. She's anxious about meeting this little human being that's been growing inside of her for months. She's not thinking of how the world is a dark, nasty, and cold place but rather how her child's presence in it will make it a much brighter and easier place. When the baby finally makes its debut, she realizes her assignment is to care for and nurture this child through life's trials and tribulations by all means necessary as the child grows into adulthood.

With my son Chris, I faced one of the toughest battles a mother could face–the threat of losing my child to gun violence. A simple move to have a chance at a better life turned into our worst nightmare. This book is my testimony of how we made it through one of the most horrifying experiences in life. There are many mothers like me who are in this unofficial club that we would have never chosen to be a part of. A club that made us feel helpless as we dealt with our children's circumstances, not knowing if they would survive their injuries or perish from them.

The news reports daily on young African-American males and females who have been killed or wounded by gun violence, and it weighs heavily on my heart. Whether they were innocent bystanders of random drive-bys, victims of police brutality, or victims of mass shootings, their families are often left shattered and confused. Then, their frustration is amplified as it feels like nothing substantial is being done to stop this type of violence from happening. We live in a society where gun violence has become increasingly regular in the United States. Depending on the state, you may encounter very lax or stringent gun laws, but either way, it still hasn't stopped the violence.

Introduction

It's important for me to share our story to help and encourage other families who are trying to put their lives back together after such a traumatic experience. I know what it's like to feel helpless and scared as your child's life drains slowly, and there is nothing you can do but trust God. Wherever you may find yourself in this process, I am a witness that God is a healer and provider. When my family was hit by this trauma, God gave me strength as I cried out to him for my son's life to be spared. My son needed to know I was being strong for him. As his mother, I needed him to FIGHT FOR HIS LIFE.

So, as I write every word and chapter of this book, I want you to understand our journey. To my son, it was unfortunate he was shot, as he refuses to live in fear. As his mother, the experience was traumatic, overwhelming, and sometimes stressful. However, it's rewarding to witness my son overcome what most may not have. He survived dire circumstances, and now I know for sure there is power in prayer.

I am no stranger to prayer. I've prayed every day for pretty much my entire life. However, there were times I felt God did not hear me and wondered if he was listening. I'm human and will admit that I once believed in instant gratification and expected God to be like a magician. However, God will make it clear what we want will not always come instantly. It will come in his timing, not ours.

Even still, He loves us enough to not leave us wondering while we wait on His timing. God often sends me encouragement through a word, a kind gesture, or even a person reciting a scripture from the Bible. And when those moments come, they are always on time.

During this time in my life, God answered my questions and prayers and made it known he was listening. He showed me in an advertently way he was here all along and working things out for our good. I had to be patient as His timing is accurate, and he knows what is best for me and my family.

Even though our family went through this experience,

Introduction

God's presence was not only known and felt by us but also by colleagues and strangers who learned of our experience. Everyone sees my son as a walking miracle and knows it was by God's grace he's still alive and here.

Our story is a story of survival and strength. It is a story of faith in God and a mother's love. You see, my son is my hero. He doesn't know it, but he is. His journey made me, along with our family, friends, colleagues, and many church members abroad, strongly believe in the power of prayer.

My desire is to help those who may be experiencing the same anguish, helplessness, and hopelessness as a parent or loved one watching their loved one fighting for their life. As you read our story, may our journey be a guiding light, as it is a remarkable testimony to tell and experience.

Chapter 1

Our Family

When I met Chris' father, Shawn, I had just moved back to Georgetown, SC, from Rhode Island after living there for two years. Shawn was visiting from Atlanta for the summer. He asked me out numerous times, and I told him no each time. Eventually, he wore me down, and I decided to go out with him. We had a nice date and continued seeing each other through the summer. We talked on the phone most days and saw each other when time permitted. At the time, Shawn's mother didn't drive, so he would drive her everywhere she needed to go. Even still, our relationship blossomed.

Meanwhile, I was looking for a job after returning home from Johnson and Wales University, but it was hard to find a good one. In Georgetown, South Carolina, getting a good-paying job was all about who you knew. The predominant jobs in Georgetown County were working at Georgetown Steel Mill or International Paper. Most of the other jobs were in restaurants, sales, or retail. If a person worked for the city or county of Georgetown, that individual was doing well financially.

My mother became frustrated with my inability to find a

stable job and told me to go live with my father, who lived in Atlanta, Georgia. So, I called my father, and he sent me the money for a bus ticket to Atlanta. When I left Georgetown, I vowed not to come back. I didn't like how my mother handled the situation. My mother called it tough love, but she wasn't encouraging or guiding me to help me figure out what to do.

I only had my learner's permit, not my driver's license. Therefore, I couldn't travel outside of Georgetown to find a better job. My job search was limited, and I had no guidance from my parents. When I moved to Atlanta to my father's place, I was on my own there too. My father left me alone during the day to figure out what to do with my life. It was during this time I found out I was pregnant with Chris. Damn!!!

One morning, I looked in the mirror and realized I looked different. My breasts looked and felt different, and my stomach was protruding a little bit. I ran into my room to look at the calendar. I counted back to when I last had my period.

I thought, "Oh no, I ain't had a period in a month. I might be pregnant."

This alarmed me because I was living with my father and was unemployed. I called Shawn to tell him. Although he was back in Atlanta, we rarely saw each other but still talked on the phone often. He was working, and I had no means to take public transportation as it was a long way from Daddy's apartment. I was not walking in the hot sun.

The furthest I walked was the neighborhood store down the street from Daddy's apartment. Even with that short distance, I would be soaking wet from the Georgia sun by the time I walked back. Some days, I walked because I craved things like pickles, Pepsi, or hot sausages, which weren't in my father's refrigerator. Once home, I would fall asleep after eating my craved snacks. I slept a lot as well. All of this was new and puzzling to me, and I wondered why I was going through this.

So, I decided to take a pregnancy test. At this point, I could barely get up to look for a job, especially dealing with all the changes I was experiencing. Without telling Daddy what was happening, I asked him to take me to the drugstore when he came home from work. He agreed, and I bought a pregnancy test and hid it where he couldn't find it.

The next day, while Daddy was at work, I took the pregnancy test. I paced the living room floor until it was time to see the results.

As I waited, I asked myself, "What am I going to do if I am pregnant? How am I going to take care of myself and a baby with no job? What will Shawn say when I tell him I'm pregnant?"

Finally, it was time to see the results. Yup, I was pregnant! I was scared and didn't know how I was going to tell Shawn and my parents I was pregnant!

I said to myself, "I am 22 years old and pregnant! How will my parents take the news? What will they say?"

I was overwhelmed with panic, worry, happiness, sadness, and, above all, fear. I was so scared my parents would think less of me, but I still needed guidance from them on what to do about my pregnancy. I was old enough to be independent but young enough to still need their direction. I also felt I let my parents down because they taught us marriage first, then children.

Despite the questions and scenarios that took over my mind, I had to find the courage to tell my parents about my pregnancy. I also felt I let God down but knew He was still with me. Knowing that gave me the courage I needed to move forward. I fell asleep feeling somewhat at ease and prepared myself to handle the outcome of the news of my pregnancy.

The next day, I called Shawn and told him I was pregnant. He asked, "So what are you going to do?

I said, "I don't know because I really don't know what to

do, and I feel like I can't have this baby knowing I can't take care of it."

We went on to talk about the options of abortion and adoption, but I decided in the end to keep my baby. Now, I still needed to tell my parents I was pregnant. I was scared out of my mind, but I had to tell them.

When I told them, it was the hardest thing for me to do because they didn't expect this from me.

I told Daddy first, and he immediately said, "You're not equipped to have a baby."

I frowned, then asked, "Why?"

He replied, "You just aren't. It's your decision to have the baby, but you can't stay here."

I was taken aback by his comment and the nonchalant manner in which he said it to me.

He said, "You need to call your mother and make plans to go back to South Carolina."

I thought to myself, "Here we go again. I'm just being shipped from parent to parent."

I called my mother and told her.

She said, "Come home, but you need to find a job."

I no longer had just myself to take care of. A baby was coming, and I needed to take care of it, too. At the time, my aunt Debbie, my mother's younger sister, worked as a security guard at International Paper.

My mother continued, "Call Debbie. She told me the Paper Mill is hiring security guards."

I replied, "OK."

In my mind, I was going to take whatever job would help me take care of myself and my baby.

Within a week, Daddy bought me a bus ticket back to Georgetown. Once there, I moved in with Aunt Debbie because my mother didn't want me to move back to her house. So, Aunt Debbie told me I could stay with her until I got a job and found my own place.

My mother and Aunt Debbie made sure I applied for the security job and helped me schedule a doctor's appointment at the Health Department near my mother and stepfather's house. I found out I was three months pregnant. I couldn't hide my pregnancy because my stomach was the biggest thing on my skinny body! Based on my examination, my estimated due date was March 16, 1993.

I still didn't know how else to feel about my pregnancy except scared. I was going to be a mother, and I could barely take care of myself. In six months, I would have a little human being depending on me to take care of them. I questioned everything because it wasn't just me anymore. I wanted to feel excited, even hopeful, but fear overwhelmed me because if I failed, I would fail myself and my baby.

Aunt Debbie trained me at her gate once I got hired as a security guard at the paper mill. The job was pretty easy, and I worked the graveyard shift. I slept during the day and was up at night. In my stomach, my baby knew to be up with me as he moved mostly at night while I was at work. Within a few months, I found a small one-bedroom apartment near my aunt Debbie's place.

We had a routine. Aunt Debbie or my mother would take me to work, and I would take a cab back home in the morning. Once home, I ate whatever I could get my hands on since I was eating for two. Most of the time, I craved hot sausages and Pepsi.

I would go to my monthly doctor's appointments at the Health Department and take pregnancy classes. My stomach was getting bigger and bigger. My baby moved more, and often played this stretching game in my stomach. When he would stretch out, his foot would protrude from different areas of my belly. Playing with him, I would push his foot back. I knew this baby was going to be a little jokester.

One day, while sitting in one of my pregnancy classes, my best friend, Elanda, was in attendance. My unborn baby decided to play his game, which caused me to take an unexpected sharp breath as my eyes got big. My instructor stopped talking and turned her attention to me.

She asked, "Are you alright?"

Instead of me explaining, I pointed to my stomach.

I said to her, "Watch carefully."

I held my shirt down so she could see what I was dealing with. She watched me gently push on my stomach as the baby stretched his feet out over and over again.

All the instructor could say was, "Oh my goodness!"

I took a deep breath and said, "The baby does this all the time. So, I gently push my stomach back in place because it is uncomfortable!"

Thank goodness, after ten minutes, he stopped moving as if he had fallen asleep. Whew! What a relief because while I loved the little game my unborn baby played, having my stomach stretched as far as possible was extremely uncomfortable. It felt like he had long feet and legs the way my stomach would stretch, and it didn't feel normal. The bigger he got in my stomach, the more anxious I became. I wanted to meet him and touch him. I couldn't wait to be a mother to this being, and the belly movement was so special to me as the day approached for us to finally meet.

The night before I went into labor, Shawn came to see me at my mother's house. Even though I was carrying one baby, I felt like it was two, as big as I was. Shawn and I discussed baby names, and I was adamant we couldn't name our baby after us. It's already confusing to have parents with the same name.

So, I told Shawn the name I chose for our son, which was Christopher Jordan. I chose "Christopher" because I wanted to name our son after my first cousin, Christian Wright. My cousin Christian, affectionately called Chris, is a year older than me and my twin sister, Dawn. We all share the same birthday and are really close to him. So, I wanted to name my firstborn after him. I wanted our baby to have Shawn's last name, but he insisted the baby have my last name. Reluctantly, I agreed.

The next day, I went into labor. My best friend, Elanda, was home and drove me to Georgetown Memorial Hospital. Elanda sat with me while I waited for Shawn and his mother to arrive.

I experienced not only regular labor pains but pains in my back as well. It was excruciatingly painful. I screamed with every contraction as I felt every pain in my back and stomach. Every hour, it felt like it was getting worse. Elanda sat scared as she witnessed what I was going through.

The nurse asked, "Would you like an epidural? It's a medicine that will ease your pain without harming the baby."

I shouted, "YES!!!"

The nurse left, and when she returned to my room, she prepared me for the epidural. I didn't see the needle at all. She told me to turn on my side, and I did as she instructed. Elanda's eyes were wide like saucers as she watched the nurse inject the epidural into my back. I didn't know the nurse had done anything because I didn't feel the needle.

Although the procedure left Elanda speechless, I felt so relieved and relaxed. I didn't feel any more pain despite the persistent contractions that followed. By this time, I couldn't wait to have the baby.

During my eleven hours of labor, I squeezed Shawn's hand and cussed at him with every contraction. Finally, I gave birth to a beautiful baby boy weighing 8 lbs., 3.9 oz. Baby Chris stared at me through the incubator while the nurse cleaned him. As we stared at one another, I wondered if he could sense my fear of being a new mother. I was amazed at how his eyes resembled his father's eyes. They were daring, questionable, and mischievous.

Once the nurse placed Chris in my arms, I didn't recall any of the earlier pain I had endured. I sat in awe at how beautiful and perfect he was. At that moment, I knew being a mother to this little human being would be an amazing adventure.

We were discharged from the hospital two days later. My mother picked us up and drove us to her house, where I stayed with her and my stepfather, Willie, for the first two weeks. I was glad to be there with them because I didn't know how to care for a newborn by myself. Aunt Debbie came over often, and I learned a lot between her and my mother.

I was grateful for a month of maternity leave from my job because it gave me priceless quality time with my infant son. When my maternity leave ended, I didn't want to leave my baby. However, I had to go back to work. My mother and Aunt Debbie helped me care for Chris while I continued to work the graveyard shift. While I worked, Chris alternated staying with my mother and Aunt Debbie. He was spoiled, to say the least.

When I got off work in the mornings, my mother or Aunt Debbie would pick me up and take Chris and I to my apartment. Once home, I would stay up for a little bit until Chris fell asleep. While he slept, I slept. Three months after Chris was born, my twin sister, Dawn, moved back to Georgetown with her son, William. They moved in with me, and since Dawn worked the day shift, she watched Chris at night and some weekends while I worked.

Shawn and his mother, Mrs. Vanderhorst, also pitched in to care for Chris. To be honest, Shawn's family was a big help. Shawn's oldest brother, Glennis, and his wife, Sandra, looked after Chris too. They were the first to welcome me and were there for me during my pregnancy and after Chris was born. I had a small family support team who helped me tremendously.

My relationship with Shawn dissolved within months of me giving birth, but we still chose to co-parent our son. Co-parenting with Shawn was rocky at first. To me, Shawn was still learning to be a father and often seemed unreliable or dependable. For instance, when I needed diapers for Chris or other assistance, Shawn's family would help us, but he was absent or delayed in his response. His unreliable behavior was consistent, and I felt like I was the only one serious about being a parent.

When Chris was seven months old, I went out on a date with a guy named Dewayne, a truck driver from Goose Creek, South Carolina. Being a single mother and dating again, I didn't want just anyone around my son. I was careful about introducing Dewayne to Chris and watched their interaction. Chris liked Dewayne right away. On our days off, Dewayne would drive down to spend time with us. He played with Chris and helped out around the apartment.

Eight months into me and Dewayne's relationship, I found out I was pregnant.

I said, "Lord Jesus! Again?"

I was about to have another baby. I had to take a minute to breathe and recollect myself and my thoughts on what to do and how to handle the situation. I just knew my mother was going to have a conniption about me having another baby and not marrying either of my children's fathers. I already had reliability issues with Shawn and did not want the problems to be repeated with Dewayne. Although Dewayne was very supportive, I questioned whether he would be a good father after the baby was born. I was also concerned about how the baby would affect our relationship.

Throughout my pregnancy, Dewayne knew about every doctor's appointment. However, he couldn't attend since his job kept him on the road. I went through my pregnancy with Dawn and Elanda being my only support system. I thought this pregnancy would have been different, but it wasn't. I began to see the same issues with Dewayne that I experienced with Shawn. I talked myself into believing it was a pregnancy mood and brushed it aside, but my frustration and annoyance continued.

I continued to focus on being a dedicated mother to my toddler, who didn't understand why or how my body was changing. Being a toddler, Chris didn't like the idea of being a big brother right away. Although I gave Chris plenty of attention, he often acted out in his toddler way, letting me know he wasn't fond of another kid invading his territory.

On Christmas day, I gave birth to my second son, Avery, which was a few months shy of Chris's 2nd birthday. After being on maternity leave for a month, I returned to the night shift because I couldn't afford daycare. So, when I got home after work, I would stay up to tend to my boys. Raising my sons was challenging yet rewarding. I had to adjust my entire routine to accommodate their needs. Chris and Avery grew closer as Chris got used to his baby brother.

My relationship with Dewayne ended after three years. Our breakup was bad, but it didn't deter Dewayne from co-parenting with me. It took some time for me to be cordial with Dewayne, but I didn't keep Avery from him. Dewayne's parents, like Shawn's, were very helpful in caring for Avery. Avery spent a lot of time with them and his older half-brothers.

One day, I had a job opportunity placed in my lap. My mother told me about an opening for an administrative specialist at Horry-Georgetown Technical College on their Georgetown campus, which would allow me to better care for my sons. I drove to the college on my day off, filled out the application, and was told I should receive a call to take a typing test. I prayed to God I would get the job. Weeks later, after successfully passing the typing test and completing the interview process, I received a letter from the college welcoming me as a new employee with my start date.

In the meantime, Chris started preschool and was so excited to go to school with his cousin, William. Each week, I received a progress report for Chris. I enjoyed his eagerness to learn new words, colors, and shapes. I also looked forward to every drawing he brought home. I helped him with his new sight words and reading books that were sent home weekly. By the end of the school year, Chris was reading short sentences. I bought more books to help my sons read and learn more words. Since Avery's birthday was late, he couldn't attend preschool for another year and a half, but he was learning right along with his big brother Chris.

I dated other guys after my breakup with Dewayne, but nothing serious. That is until I met Devron, a divorced father of a five-year-old, while working at the college. He asked me out numerous times, but I turned him down. He was persistent. Whenever he saw me, he asked me out. So, finally, I gave in and told him yes.

I thought, "No harm in going out on one date."

After the first date, we continued to see each other. Turned out our mothers grew up in the same community, our grandparents were members of the same church, and my stepfather and his parents were classmates.

My sons liked him, and they were comfortable around him. It was important they be comfortable in his presence, as I didn't know how far or where our relationship was going. Further on in our relationship, we discussed having more children, which led to us agreeing on the importance of having safe sex. We even went to the store to buy condoms because we desired to avoid pregnancy.

Weeks later, I felt nauseous and lightheaded. I glanced at my pocket calendar and realized I had missed my period. I drove to the store, purchased a pregnancy test, and went home to take it. I was pregnant for the third time! With the pregnancy test in my hand, I drove to Devron's apartment and told him we were having a baby. He was so ecstatic about having another baby and wanted to make plans for us as a family. Relieved by his reaction, I was just as happy to have another baby added to the bunch. I always wanted a big family, as my parents were from large families. I came from a big, blended family, so it seemed I would have one as well.

Yet this news was my sister's cue to move into her own place. Dawn and I still helped each other with our kids. However, after finding out I was pregnant with my third baby, she began to look for a home for her and William.

It wasn't long before Dawn found an apartment a few minutes from where we lived. If it was up to my twin sister and I, we would live together for the rest of our lives. We didn't depend on each other but were used to being there for one another. We're twins! We were raised to be there for each other, and that's what we did. It felt weird after my sister moved to a place of her own. It took a little while for us to feel normal living in separate homes, but our sons were still close like brothers.

The boys were waiting to see if I would have a boy or a girl. Avery told me I was having a girl and that she was going to be his baby! Chris was already used to being a big brother, so a new baby wasn't as exciting since he was the oldest. My nephew William was also unphased and saw it as another kid to play with since he was the oldest.

During the months of my pregnancy, Devron and I had some challenges in our relationship. These were questionable challenges that I overlooked since we both were determined to be a family. The day I gave birth to our baby girl, Brianna, who we nicknamed "Bri," Devron and I were on a break from each other. During this time, I focused on my children, not him.

However, months after giving birth, Devron asked me to marry him, and I accepted. We both agreed to get married at the Georgetown County Courthouse and have a small wedding reception because we wanted to buy a house. In December 1999, a few weeks before Bri's 1st birthday, we got married and had a lovely reception afterward.

Devron and I rented a house for our blended family a few

weeks later and stayed there for a year. We purchased our first home a year later. Even with the adjustments of our new blended family and moving to a new home, Chris and Avery thrived in school. They often visited and spent time with their fathers, maintaining a relationship with the other side of their families. However, I noticed that this brought about changes in Devron.

The more time the boys spent with their other families, the less and less Devron engaged with Chris and Avery. This caused tension between me and both boys' fathers. It also caused friction in our marriage. Devron became controlling and started to criticize and dominate me through intimidation and manipulation, which made me question and doubt myself. For instance, he would tell me what clothing to wear even though I dressed modestly. If I had errands to run, he required me to tell him where I was going. Then, he would follow me to these places to make sure I went there.

Eventually, his abuse became physical. In anger, he pushed and slammed me into things, which resulted in several injuries. He was verbally, mentally, and physically abusive, which made it unbearable to stay in our marriage. Chris and Avery heard the arguments and witnessed the abuse I experienced, and it left them feeling helpless. Brianna was too young to know what was going on, not to mention Devron masked his abusive behavior by being a loving father toward her. After four years of marriage, I filed for divorce.

Chapter 2

The Younger Years

Chris was a smart kid. He was an average student, but he loved to play basketball. Like most kids, he dreamed of playing for the NBA. However, I encouraged Chris to have a backup plan. Being a concerned mother, I wanted Chris to think beyond sports. So, I told him if plan A didn't work, then go with plan B, and so on, until he reached the goals he set for himself.

Nevertheless, I signed him up to play recreational basketball, and he began to learn the sport. He was not a good player at first, but the more he played, the more he learned, and the more he loved the sport. Towards the end of the basketball season, the league held an All-Star game, where the good players were chosen to play in the tournament. However, Chris was not picked.

My father always told us, "Whatever career you choose, make sure you are the best."

Just as my father told me and my siblings, I made sure Chris got the same impartation of wisdom. While it hurt Chris that he wasn't chosen, it motivated him to practice even harder. He practiced every day, determined to be on the all-star team the next basketball season. And sure enough, Chris was selected for the all-star team each year after that.

I watched him flourish as a good basketball player. He went on to play basketball for middle school and high school. To watch him play basketball, he made it seem easy, and his moves were graceful. It was a team effort to make sure Chris was at every practice and game. My mother and sister helped. My high school friend Stephanie and her family did as well. Jasmar, Stephanie's son, and Chris were best friends, and both played basketball together. Going to his games was a family affair because we all loved to watch Chris play.

Although I enjoyed being a basketball mom, I decided to go back to college to finish my bachelor's degree. Due to my work schedule, I was unable to sit in a classroom. Online classes had become popular for working people. So, I applied to the University of Maine at Augusta and was accepted into their Library Science program.

Life was hectic between the kids, Chris' basketball schedule, and my college classes. A new relationship was far from my mind. However, one day, while walking back to my desk at work, a really tall man walked through the door. As he entered the office, he had to duck down so his head wouldn't hit the doorway.

I asked myself, "How tall is this dude?"

Then, without thinking, I blurted out, "Can I help you? You don't belong here, and how tall are you?"

He laughed and explained, "I'm looking for information on the fall classes for me and my sister."

I replied, "OK, and what's your name?"

He said, "Romonto, but everyone calls me Money. Oh yeah, and I'm 6'9"."

I asked, "Our counselors can help with that. Would you like to speak with them?"

He replied, "Yes."

So, I introduced him to one of our counselors. Once his meeting was finished, he came back to my office to thank me.

He said, "Me and my sister will definitely be back to take classes once we complete the paperwork."

After Money and his sister Quonda began classes at the college, I saw them regularly, and a friendship began between all three of us. My friendship with Money blossomed into a relationship. At first, Money didn't believe I had kids, even though I mentioned them all the time. He met Chris first and then Avery. Just like me, my sons were amazed at how tall he was.

There's a fourteen-year age gap between Money and I. He was by far the youngest person I had ever dated. My relationship with Money gave me stability, which was something I never had with other men. He genuinely loved my children, and they loved him in return. Our relationship was beautiful and loving.

I was finally in a good place in my life to have this wonderful relationship. Money and I were committed to each other, and for once, I didn't fear abuse or inconsistent behavior from him. He showed me love, kindness, and compassion because he knew what I went through in my previous relationships and marriage.

Depending on his work schedule, Money did his best to attend every basketball game, cook for us, give the kids sound advice, and talk about sports. The kids grew fond of him over the years and approved his marriage proposal. They called him their stepdad even though we were not married but lived together, raising three children.

Over the years, Money and I continued to go through milestones with the children. They filled our lives with father-daughter dances, banquets, family reunions, proms, and high school and boot camp graduations. Our proudest moment was when each of the children graduated from high school.

Together, we watched them grow into mature young adults deciding their next endeavors in life.

The kids had their own growing pains, but Chris was the main one going through it while in high school. Our trying moments as parents were the two times in life when Chris got into trouble. Once, when he was a teenager, Chris witnessed one of his friends threaten a guy. The police considered Chris guilty by association since he was standing there with his friend.

The police came to my house looking for Chris, handcuffed him, and took him to the police department for questioning. His friend was charged and transferred to the detention center because he committed the offense. When Money and I picked up Chris from the police station, I yelled at my son because he was never in trouble, and he was now a teenager, not this cute little kid anymore.

I questioned why Chris was hanging with this "so-called" friend who got him in trouble. I told him numerous times about how African American boys and young men are seen in society and by the police. Although he hadn't experienced the unfair treatment, it still exists. I was disappointed in him. I felt he was gullible with the type of friends he was hanging around.

I was harder on Chris than Avery and Brianna because they didn't make me question them as individuals or question the kind of friends they were around.

I always told my kids, "Be careful with calling someone who gets you in trouble a friend. Not everyone is your friend."

When Chris was younger, his punishments would be to answer questions from a history book I had or have his action figures or video games taken away. That was lenient compared to the punishment I had for him getting into this trouble. No hanging out with friends, no video games, only going places with me or Money, no cell phone, no personal life!

Chris participated in a Juvenile Diversion Program for a

couple of months and did community service. He remained on punishment for a while. After completing the program, the charges were dismissed and expunged from Chris' record. He learned so much being in the program and earned my trust back. Whatever I told Chris, Money backed me up as he didn't want Chris to get into unnecessary trouble.

Money and I decided to move to Litchfield Beach, a section of Pawleys Island. Avery and Bri transferred to schools on Pawleys Island. However, Chris remained at Georgetown High School until his senior year. Chris said he wanted a change of scenery, so we transferred him to Waccamaw High School. I was unsure if he'd blend in, but to my surprise, Chris did well at his new school.

Towards the end of his senior year, Chris didn't have a strategic plan in place for his life after graduation. Outside of basketball, Chris was stuck when it came to finding a good career. Even though he was young, Chris actively tried to figure out his life. I told him his options were the military, moving out on his own, or going to college. Since he didn't have money to move out and wasn't interested in the military, he applied and was accepted at Horry Georgetown Technical College, where I worked.

Chris did well and finally found a job at Dollar General down the street from where we lived. Chris was showing us he was a responsible young man. One day, I noticed he wasn't going to work and asked him about his job. He told me he was fired.

I could feel Chris' answer was going to frustrate me, so I asked him, "Why did you get fired?"

He said, "I was let go because I didn't pay for the food I was eating. I was hungry and didn't have any money."

Before he could explain everything to me, I reiterated to him the circumstances of being a young African American man. I know he dismissed my frustration and concerns as his mother. My children sometimes felt I overreacted, but I had reason to be concerned as they were becoming young adults. Not too long after he lost his job, the unthinkable happened. Chris was arrested for forgery.

I love my son, but this time he made a bad decision. When he got arrested, Money and I were in the process of moving from a three-bedroom condo to a two-bedroom townhouse. As we were moving, Chris told me he was going to hang out with one of his friends. I received a call an hour later from a deputy with the Georgetown Detention Center informing me they had my son in custody. They said he forged someone's signature on two checks.

The deputy was really nice as she explained to me when he would appear in court, along with other information. She then allowed me to speak with Chris. The anger, frustration, and concern I felt in that moment was because I took this personally. I never wanted any of my children to get in trouble like this. I sacrificed a lot to raise them. For one of my children to do something this stupid was a slap in my face.

I didn't know what to say when Chris got on the phone.

Without thinking, I yelled, "So you had to go to jail! What were you thinking? Did you hear anything I've been telling you?"

The only thing Chris could say to me was, "No, ma'am. I wasn't thinking. I'm sorry, Mama."

"You damn right! You're a young adult now," I blurted.

I was so angry and disappointed in him. However, I was worried about him being in jail as he had never been incarcerated before. My skinny young adult son was locked up with people who committed worse crimes than him. I worried about him the whole time he was there.

I waited a few days to call my father about Chris. Once I told my father all that happened, he wasn't mad, but my father was disappointed.

He told me, "Let him sit in there. While he's there, he'll learn he and will never go to jail ever again in his life."

My father rarely gave me pep talks.

He continued, "Don't blame yourself. You raised good kids. Chris just made a dumb mistake. Now, let him learn his lesson. And trust me, he will learn his lesson."

Chris' hearing was set for a couple of months later. Reluctantly, I let Chris sit in jail for a month and a half. My parents had the money to pay for Chris' bond but chose not to bail him out. They wanted him to understand what he did was wrong and not go back to jail ever again in his life.

I wrote to him daily and included bible verses in my letters. I showed him tough love, but I still loved my son. I sincerely wanted him to learn this hard lesson in life. He was a good kid but made a bad decision that could've cost him his freedom. Money and I visited him on weekends because he was only allowed two days for visitation - Tuesdays and Saturdays.

I mentally prepared myself for going to the jail on Saturdays since I was only allowed a 30-minute visit with Chris. Once we signed in and showed our ID, we waited to be called back to see him. As we sat there, I observed the long line of incarcerated men being escorted in to visit with their relatives or loved ones.

Eventually, I spotted my son as he walked towards the glass where we sat. I looked him over to make sure he was alright and asked him questions as I was concerned for his wellbeing. I had to find out everything I could within those short 30 minutes. Once he returned to his cell, I wouldn't see him again until the following Saturday. I felt helpless and blamed myself for his actions because I loved my son that much. I prayed that I made the right decision by letting him stay in jail to learn this hard lesson.

One day, a female deputy from the jail called me out of the blue.

She said, "I am one of the deputies assigned to Chris. I want to encourage you to be strong. Your son doesn't belong in jail, and he is not a troublemaker. I knew that from the first moment he came in here. We talk every day, and I remind him that he has someone here that cares for him. He's angry about being here and not being bailed out. But I remind him that his actions got him here. I do want you to know that he is showing signs of remorse. Don't give up on him, and stay encouraged."

I thanked her for calling me as tears quietly rolled down my face. After we hung up, I cried as I could no longer contain my emotions.

Every week, I called and gave my father an update on Chris, Avery, and Bri. One Sunday in December 2013, I called my father to provide an update. I shared with him that Avery had finished school in the Navy, and we were all looking forward to the Christmas holidays.

He said, "How's Chris?"

I shared with him the conversation I had with the deputy. My father then told me a story about his time in reform school. Over the years, my father mentioned that he was sent to reform school but never shared why until this moment.

After finishing the story, my father said, "Shawn, you are a good mother. You have never asked me or your mother for anything, and I'm proud of you."

I said, "Thank you, daddy. You know, Avery is coming home for the holidays. We're going to call you once he arrives."

My father was looking forward to talking to the kids.

The last thing he said was, "Alright, let me get to my ironing. I'll talk to you soon."

I didn't know that would be my last conversation with my father.

A few days later, while at work, I got a message from my cousin, Bootsie, asking me to call her as soon as possible. I thought it was odd because the only time we heard from our father's side was if something happened. Knowing our aunts and father were older and sickly, we knew the unexpected could happen to any of them. I was hoping not to hear any bad news about my relatives. I called her back but wasn't prepared for what she had to say. I screamed and then cried so hard as she told me my father was found dead in his apartment.

One of my colleagues heard me scream and came running to my desk.

Shaking in shock, I said, "My father died."

My colleagues tried to comfort and calm me down, especially Eileen, who I worked with for 16 years. She was about to leave to go home when one of my colleagues stopped her to let her know what had happened. She practically ran back into the building to find me surrounded by everyone as I cried uncontrollably. All I thought about was my father and that he was no longer with me. Eileen slowly sat down in front of me.

Sternly, she said, "Shawn, focus on me."

She continued to talk to me calmly until I calmed down and stopped shaking. She didn't leave until she knew I was calm enough to drive to my mother and stepfather's house.

Once I arrived at my parents' house, plans were made for me and my siblings to travel to Atlanta. At the time of his death, my father had worked for Delta Airlines for 46 years. His supervisor helped schedule our flights and gave me information about his insurance. She walked me through what I never thought I would be doing - planning my father's memorial.

In the midst of making our travel plans, my mother looked at me.

She said, "It's time for Chris to get out of jail. If we're all going to Atlanta to say our final goodbyes, so should Chris."

The day after Avery came home from Chicago, my mother gave my nephew, William, and Avery the bail money for Chris. Meanwhile, Dawn and I flew to Atlanta. Once the bond was paid, Avery and William waited for Chris outside the jail.

When Chris walked out and sat in the car, the first thing Chris asked was, "Where's Mama?"

Chris was not aware of my father's passing. So, Avery and William told him where I was and what had happened to my father. Immediately, he called me to ask how I was doing. At the time, Myself, Dawn, and our brother, Brucie, were on the way to the morgue.

I calmly answered Chris, "I'm not OK. This was a shock to all of us. Right now, we are on our way to the morgue. But I am happy you're out of jail. I need you, Avery, and Bri to prepare to come to Atlanta. I'll give you more details later."

Within days of our arrival in Atlanta, we arranged for Daddy's belongings to go to charity, and mementos of him were split between me, Dawn, Brucie, and our children. Most of the grandkids drove to Atlanta to say their final goodbyes to their beloved grandfather. However, Brucie's kids were unable to attend as it was two days after Christmas, and the flights were expensive.

After Daddy's memorial, Chris stayed at my mother's house for a year, helping with my stepfather, who was bedridden. During his stay, he participated in a program to expunge his record. Once the charges were expunged from his record, Chris was finally able to get a job at Lowe's Foods as a stocker. Later on, he transitioned to Walmart.

Chris was so happy to get his life back on track. He apologized to me for all that happened and said he had learned a valuable lesson. My father's words came to mind, and I thanked God for my son finally understanding his actions had consequences. He's a young man who can be or do anything he wants to do in life.

A year later, Chris and my nephew William moved into an apartment in Georgetown, South Carolina. They agreed to live there for a year and then relocate to the prospective places they desired to go. Chris would move to Atlanta, Georgia, and William would move to the state of Virginia.

Chris was doing well, but he wanted more for himself. He felt if he stayed in Georgetown, he'd only be working dead-end jobs. He knew there were more opportunities in life for a young person like him. He learned from his mistakes and looked forward to a fresh start. I watched my son earn my trust back and grow as a person.

After talking to his best friend Darius, Chris believed his fresh start would be in Columbia, South Carolina. Darius and Chris talked daily, and Chris shared how frustrated he was with not finding a decent job in Georgetown.

Darius told Chris, "Jobs in Columbia are plentiful. If you move here, you can easily find something until you find the right job for you. Trust me, you will definitely find a job here with no problem."

After their conversation, Chris decided Columbia would be a good fit for him and his goals. He notified the rental agency that he would not renew his apartment lease and packed up his belongings. In May 2016, Chris moved to Columbia. Within a week of his move, Chris found a job at a landscaping company and worked there until September. Then, he was hired as a stocker for Walmart.

Chris liked his job. He called me every week, usually on his way to work. It was his way of checking in on Bri and I while asking me questions about cooking. To be honest, it felt odd that Chris was two hours away from home. I remember feeling the same way when Avery left for boot camp.

My kids were slowly leaving, and the empty nest made me feel anxious, something I was not used to. After becoming a mother, my kids were my life. But now it was time I focused on my own goals. This was weird! While still adjusting to my father's death, I had to adjust to both my sons not being home. It was too much.

Although Brianna was still in high school and home, I was

slowly trying to figure out what I was going to do for myself. That was scary for me because I didn't know where to start. During our talks, Chris told me he was saving money to move into his own place and get a car of his own. He sounded so happy and optimistic about his current goals, and for once, he felt very independent.

Chapter 3

Who Did This to You

Thursday, January 26, 2017, was an ordinary day for me and my kids. This was Brianna's last year in high school, so this year was going to be different. She was the last of my children to graduate, and I was indeed a proud mom. Avery was stationed in San Diego and doing very well out there. Chris worked and lived in Columbia.

As I drove to work, my thoughts of the day were my class assignments from my graduate program that started earlier in the week. I brainstormed the topics I wanted to write for my project, the modules I needed to print for the class, and additional requirements.

I could not wait until I got off from my job because I needed to work on my topic proposal. In late September 2015, I started an online graduate history program through Southern New Hampshire University (SNHU). I finished a course a week earlier, and I was able to look at the next class's content and modules. Once I arrived at my job, I narrowed down the topics for my project. My love for history and research led me to SNHU. It gave me a deeper understanding of people, collecting data, and interpretation of the past.

Researching information took hard work, persistence, and, above all, time.

Also, this was the week I watched a three-part series of my favorite R&B group, New Edition, with my former college roommate, China. We commentated as we viewed each episode. We had fun texting each other about the series. I met China at Johnson and Wales University over twenty years ago, and we've been best friends ever since. My kids know her as "Aunt China." Even though she lives in New York, she knows every aspect of my children's lives. She watched them grow up from a distance. You would think she lived in South Carolina as much as we communicated.

China and I were having so much fun watching the last episode of the series. I managed to finish a page of my topic proposal at the same time. We ended our call by telling each other we would talk again soon. She knew I was in graduate school, maintaining an "A" GPA while working full-time. I was so proud of myself, but it was getting late, and I had to get up early for work. So, I took allergy medicine to help me sleep through the sinus issues that developed while we were on the phone. The medicine ensured I could breathe and wouldn't wake up in the middle of the night to blow my nose.

My phone rang as I started to climb the stairs to our bedroom, where Money was watching TV. The call was from Darius, Chris' best friend. I answered, but the call dropped as I continued up the stairs. It was weird, and I thought maybe Darius' cell phone had mistakenly butt-dialed me. Once in my room, I called Darius back, unprepared for what I was about to hear next!

Darius said, "Hey, Ms. Shawn. I'm calling to tell you Chris was shot in his leg."

Confused, I asked, "Chris was shot in his leg? What!!! Where? How?"

Darius replied, "Yes, ma'am. He was shot on his way home, but we're at the hospital right now. He is fine, Ms.

Shawn. Don't worry, he's fine. They took him in the back to look at him."

Although I wanted to trust what he told me, it felt suspicious that he kept saying Chris was fine.

I went along and simply replied, "OK."

I could hear someone talking to Darius in the background.

Finally, Darius said, "Ms. Shawn, the nurse wants to talk to you."

The nurse got on the phone, and the conversation began to confirm my suspicion.

The nurse asked, "Are you Christopher Wright's mother?"

I responded, "Yes, I am. How is my son?"

She said, "I am not able to tell you that over the phone. Can you come to the hospital right now?"

I could feel for sure now that there was more to the story than what I was being told.

Trying to remain calm, I said, "Ma'am, I don't live in Columbia. I live in Pawleys Island. I am at least two hours away from Columbia."

Concerned, she said, "Oh my! OK, umm. Well, although I'm not able to go into detail, I will let you know your son is being transported to Palmetto Richland."

"Why?" I asked.

She explained, "Palmetto Richland is more equipped to deal with gunshot wound victims."

I said, "OK. Well, what hospital is he at right now?"

She replied, "He's at Palmetto Baptist."

Since she told me Chris was being moved, I thought I might circle back to my original question.

So, I asked again, "How is my son doing?"

I believed the nurse was now more inclined to share additional details with me since I was coming from out of town.

This time, she answered me and said, "The only thing I can tell you is his vital signs are shaky. I am going to give you the address to Palmetto Health, and when you get there, go to the EMERGENCY Room. Go over to the registration desk and let them know your name. Inform them your son was admitted, and a hospital liaison will come out to give you an update on your son's prognosis."

I wrote down the information she gave and thanked her.

As I hung up the phone, perplexed, I looked at Money and said, "Chris was shot in his leg, and he's being transported to another hospital."

Trying to hold it together, I continued, "Something isn't right. I need to get to Chris NOW!"

I think the urgency in my voice caused Money to move faster. He got up from the recliner and started packing his clothes, thinking Chris being shot may not be life-threatening but still questionable.

I turned in a daze, opened my closet door, and started throwing clothes out of my closet onto our bed.

Money asked, "How long do you think we will be in Columbia?"

I replied, "I don't know."

Since he did not know how to pack, Money packed enough clothes for the weekend. However, I packed for the week because I felt I would be there longer.

I kept saying over and over in my head, "I need to get to Chris. I need to get to Chris. He needs to know his mother is on the way. God, please let him feel I am on my way to him. Chris shouldn't be alone in the hospital room. He needs me."

I replayed in my mind what the nurse told me. I did not like the nurse telling me his vital signs were shaky. I had questions, and I didn't like this feeling at all. It just didn't seem right. Like there was more to it, and it was bad.

Then I thought, "Darius knew someone had shot Chris in the leg at the time of the phone call. Maybe he has more details he could not share over the phone."

I mentally recalled my son's daily routine as I continued to pack my clothes. Chris didn't have a car and relied on public transportation to get to work, which meant he walked to and from the bus stop daily. I didn't mind him walking to the bus stop in the daytime, but I was more worried about him walking home at night. Even though Chris lived in Columbia, he was still unfamiliar with the neighborhoods. There are certain neighborhoods in Columbia a person who is new to the area should avoid.

The neighborhood Chris lived in was decent, but some streets were not. Chris had no choice but to walk from the bus stop alone at night, and I felt that wasn't a safe thing to do. Regardless, walking at night has never felt safe to me. Even where I live, I don't walk at night. When Chris told me he walked ten minutes from the bus stop at night, I prayed daily for him to get home unharmed. I knew it was the only way for Chris because he had no other transportation. Routinely, he walked from the bus stop with no problem.

As I threw the final pieces of clothing I needed on the bed, my heart remembered my last conversation with Chris earlier that morning. Chris called me while waiting at the bus stop. Once on the bus, we talked and laughed like usual. We talked about his week and the apartment he was interested in. Then, it wasn't long before the bus stopped near his job.

He got off the bus, and before he walked to his job, I said, "I love you. Be careful."

He said, "OK, Mama. I love you too."

After we hung up, God compelled me to pray for him. Without hesitation, I prayed for God to guide his steps, keep him safe, and for no harm to come his way. I obediently listened to God without questioning or wondering why I was doing so.

Money and I were finally ready to leave for Columbia. I called Avery to tell him about Chris but got his voicemail. I didn't want to leave a message saying someone had shot his brother. So, I called my best friend Virginia, one of my high school classmates. I told her what happened and explained that I needed to speak with Avery but couldn't get in touch with him.

I was unsure whether or not the Navy would send Avery home, but I needed him to know what was going on with his brother. Avery was stationed at a naval base in San Diego. Virginia lived in San Diego, near the naval base. She assured me not to worry. She would have her husband Chris drive to the naval base to find out Avery's whereabouts.

I texted my other best friends, Kena, Elanda, and Deborah, as it was late. I knew they would see my text once they got up for work. By then, I'd have more information to share.

Money drove because I had taken Benadryl earlier in the evening and was in no condition to drive. Not to mention, my nerves were completely shot. Ironically, I did not feel sleepy at all. I guess because of my adrenaline. It was the longest drive to Columbia I had ever experienced in my life!

My goal was to get to my son. Chris needed to know his mother was there. I didn't want Chris to be alone without his family. Darius was there, but he could only do so much because he wasn't an immediate family member, even though we felt he was a part of our family.

Money tried to calm my nerves by reassuring me that Chris was in good hands at the hospital. He had checked the hospital reviews prior to us leaving for Columbia. Although Money tried to reassure me, it didn't work.

All I could do was look out the car window and think, "You're not driving fast enough."

Even though he was going 65 or 70 mph, it felt like he was driving the speed limit, or maybe he was speeding. I didn't know for sure. I just needed to get to my son.

I thought and prayed, at the same time, "Please God, please let Chris be OK. Please."

We arrived in Columbia a little after four in the morning. I did what the nurse instructed me to do. I went to the desk, informed them who I was, and stated why I was there.

The nurse at the desk made a phone call and, after hanging up, replied, "Mr. Johnson will be down to see you in thirty minutes."

We took a seat in the waiting area. My nerves were on edge as we waited.

Internally, I prayed, "Please let there be good news. I don't think I can deal with any bad news. Please, God, don't let Mr. Johnson tell me any bad news about Chris. He has to be OK!"

I envisioned a scenario in which they wheeled Chris out, and I could take him home. Instead, I heard a voice calling my name. As Mr. Johnson walked over to me and Money, I snapped back into reality.

He said, "Ms. Wright, I am Mr. Johnson, the hospital liaison. I'm going to take you to the surgical floor. Please come with me."

As we walked, Mr. Johnson shared, "Chris was shot three times. He just got out of surgery and is being admitted to Palmetto Health."

Confused, I looked at Mr. Johnson and said, "I was told he was shot in his leg. Where did the three shots come from?"

Mr. Johnson looked over his notes and replied, "He was shot three times, and he's doing fine."

He didn't tell me where he was shot, so I assumed the three shots were in different places on Chris' leg. We finally reached the surgical floor of the hospital.

Mr. Johnson said, "I'm going back to check on Chris' prognosis and will return to let you know what I've learned."

Confused, I looked at Money and tried to comprehend all Mr. Johnson told us.

I said, "Chris was shot three times. THREE TIMES! Huh?"

Money was at a loss for words.

It wasn't long before Mr. Johnson returned, but he wasn't alone. A doctor accompanied him to speak with us. The look on her face told me it was not good news.

The doctor said, "Chris is not doing well, and we're taking him back to surgery because he is bleeding internally. To stop the bleeding, we need to administer numerous blood transfusions and platelets. The first twenty-four to forty-eight hours are crucial for him to survive his injuries."

I felt my face turn red as my body started shaking. I could tell by the look on the doctor's face and my reaction that I wasn't taking the news well. It was like I was having an out-of-body experience.

The doctor emphasized, "I am going to do all in my power to save your son."

I nodded my head in acknowledgment of her words. After the doctor left, I collapsed in the chair next to Money and cried, hiding my face inside his jacket. It was the only place I felt safe from the peering eyes of those around us.

Money tried to be strong for me as I wept for my son, but I knew he was just as hurt. All he could do was hold me tight with his long arms. He didn't have to say a word because his embrace said it all. He helped me raise my children and loved them as his own. What happened to Chris hurt him as well.

The nearby security guard saw the interaction and brought over a box of tissues.

She said, "I don't know you and don't know how dire your son's situation is, but I am praying for you all."

I replied, "Thank you," as I reached for the box of tissues and took some out to blow my nose.

I knew my eyes were red from crying so hard. After I mustered enough strength to stand, I told Money I was going to the bathroom. After the security guard directed me down the hall to the bathroom, I walked in and locked the door behind me. I turned on the faucet to wash my face. As I looked at myself in the mirror, I saw the sadness, hurt, confusion, and helplessness that ran rapidly within me.

I sat on the toilet and cried out to God, "Please spare my son. Please don't let Chris die. Please guide the doctor's hands to heal him. Please, I can't lose Chris like I lost Daddy. Losing Daddy was hard, but if I lost my son to gun violence, it would be unbearable for me. Please don't let me lose my son. Please, God. Please hear my prayers, God. Please. What am I going to tell Avery and Bri? Please don't let it be this way, please. Please, God, I know you hear me. Please don't let him die. Please. I love you, God, and I know you will take care of him. He's in your hands, but I feel so helpless. Please don't let him die. Please."

After that, I couldn't cry anymore. I felt so tired like my body was drained of its energy. I needed to be strong for Chris, but I didn't feel strong. I felt so weak and tired, but I believed God heard me. No, I was confident He heard my prayers.

I took several deep breaths before leaving the bathroom. Then, I called Shawn, Chris' father, once I returned to the waiting area. It was hard telling him what happened to Chris and what Mr. Johnson and his doctor told us. Shawn just broke down, and I did my best to console him. The last time I heard Shawn cry like that was in 2001 when his mother passed away. I couldn't cry anymore. I had already cried so much and prayed so hard. I needed to be strong for my family now. Besides, I felt it was important for Shawn to have this moment to process what was happening because it was a lot.

I believe he was a devastated father who feared the worst, which was losing his oldest son to gun violence. When I told Shawn that Chris had to go back to surgery because of internal bleeding, I felt his pain because I, too, was in pain. I believed what might have hurt Shawn the most was hearing the hurt and sadness in my voice as I relayed the details of Chris' condition from the doctor and Mr. Johnson.

I didn't have all the answers to the questions Shawn asked. Shawn is a very inquisitive person, and I felt he always asked questions about everything. But at that moment, I could only tell him what was told to me. I didn't have a notepad like a journalist or recordings from my cell phone with details about the shooting, the whereabouts, and what happened to Chris. I couldn't answer his questions because I didn't know! The only thing I knew was Chris wasn't doing well and had to return to surgery after just having surgery. It was imperative Shawn made it to Palmetto Hospital to see Chris alive.

After I ensured Shawn was alright, we hung up the phone so he could make plans to come to the hospital. I went to the bathroom multiple times. Money said both of us had bubble guts. You know, when your stomach feels queasy, and you have no appetite, but you feel you still need to use the bathroom. Well, that's how we felt as we sat and waited for hours.

It was dark when we first arrived at the hospital, but daylight was breaking. I looked out at the city below from the hospital window and watched people walk and cars drive by. It appeared to be a normal day. The only thing was, it wasn't normal for me as there was an uncertainty of how it would end and whether my son would live or not.

Chris' second surgery took a long time. While we waited to hear from his doctor, I called my mother and twin sister, Dawn, to tell them what happened. They were shocked and asked what they could do to help. What I needed most from them was to tell the rest of our family because I couldn't make all those calls. I was focused on finding my son Avery's whereabouts.

Dawn said, "I'll go to your house to help with Bri. Once I get Christian off to school, I'll stay there until you call with further instructions."

It was hard as a mother to be so far away from my military child. As a new military family, we were slowly getting used to Avery living 3000 miles away. Being in the Navy, Avery was always out at sea. We weren't permitted to know his whereabouts for security reasons. However, this was one of those times that I wished I could just override protocol and call him up. I didn't want him reading this news on social media. I needed to get in touch with him before Chris' friends began posting about what happened.

Sure enough, a couple of friends started the "Say a prayer for Dub!" post. Chris' friends called him "Dub" because of his laid-back personality. He very seldom spoke unless needed. After Chris' shooting, a few of his friends took to social media in disbelief and shock because they knew his character. Darius stepped in and made them take down their posts and explained that Avery had not been notified, and I didn't want him finding out through a social media post.

Meanwhile, Virginia called and said her husband went to the Navy base to find out information on how to locate Avery. Her husband was given the number to the American Red Cross so they could find Avery and share the information regarding Chris.

Virginia said, "I will call you back once I have more information. I got you, sis! You just stay focused and continue to be strong for Chris. Don't worry. We'll handle things here in San Diego."

I felt so much better because I knew my friend, and she would ensure it was handled. I then called my supervisor, Peggy, to let her know what happened.

She asked, "How long will you be there?"

I firmly said, "I don't know, as long as I need to be here. I'm not leaving my son."

At that moment, my job didn't matter, only Chris'. I am a mother first and an employee second. After my conversation with Peggy, I remembered what my mother taught me.

She said, "Shawn, a mother's main priority is her children."

Chris was my main priority, and finding Avery was my other priority. It was important for me to get in touch with Avery. With all that was happening, I needed to speak with him and know he was OK. Finally, Virginia called back with the American Red Cross on a three-way call.

The representative with the Red Cross said, "We will locate Avery and let his superiors know about Chris' prognosis. We need your permission to obtain Chris' medical report from Palmetto Richland Hospital so we can forward it to Avery's superiors."

I replied, "You have my permission to access Chris' medical reports."

I was so relieved the organization helped us find Avery because I needed him to come home and help me with this crisis. I didn't know if Chris was going to live or die. Money sat right next to me, praying for Chris, but I still needed Avery there so they both could help keep me calm. Anxiety set in, and I felt my blood pressure going up the more I thought about everything. I never expected to face something like this.

AFTER HOURS OF WAITING FOR CHRIS' surgery to finish, his doctor walked into the waiting area. I prayed he wouldn't die on the operating table. I could feel my heart in my throat as she walked closer to Money and I. I looked at her carefully, bracing myself for the news she was about to give us. Then I noticed the smile on her face.

I shouted internally, "Thank you, Jesus! Thank you, God, for your grace and mercy! Thank you! Yes, Lord, he survived!"

Before she uttered a word, her smile assured me Chris had survived the surgery. The doctor walked over to us and proceeded with the update on Chris' progress.

She said, "Chris' surgery was successful, but he is not out of the woods yet. We found five holes in his intestines, which needed to be plugged. If we try to plug all the holes at once, Chris will die of septic shock. It's best for us to operate every few days so his body has time to heal from each procedure. These surgeries are life-threatening, and he could have died from the two surgeries already performed today, but he didn't. Also, we need to give Chris more blood and platelets because he lost a lot of blood between the incident and surgeries."

The doctor paused to make sure Money and I were keeping up with what she had said so far.

Then she continued, "Also, Chris' head and eyes are swollen from the transfusions and platelets he's already received. Please understand that when you walk into Chris' room, he will not look like himself. It won't be a pretty sight. He is in an induced coma and on a ventilator. Again, I'm doing everything in my power to save your son. As soon as they get his room ready, you can go and see him."

The doctor's news brought me some reassurance. She was genuine and nice, and I honestly believed she was doing everything possible to ensure Chris survived his wounds.

It was at least another hour before Chris' room was ready, which gave me time to share the news with my mother and sister. They both kept my extended family informed because I was still unable to call anyone. I wasn't mentally ready for multiple phone calls and just wanted to see Chris. I needed him to know I was here.

After I hung up with them, I called Shawn and updated him with the doctor's progress report.

I said, "We're now waiting to see Chris. They will let us know once his room is ready."

Shawn replied, "OK, I'm going to share the news with my kids. They'll want to know how their big brother is doing. I'm also going to tell the rest of my family."

Shawn had four other children. Chris was just as close to his siblings on his father's side as he was to Avery and Bri. As a blended family, it was important to me for all the children to love each other and be there for one another. I came from a blended family, and I love all my siblings.

Shawn said, "I need to get things situated here in Atlanta. As soon as I'm done, I'll drive to the hospital. I'll let you know once I leave, but I need to call my kids first."

Shawn sounded so sad and hurt, but he tried to stay strong for not only his kids but for Chris, too. I knew how he felt. That uncertainty that comes with praying and hoping for the best. Our son was not out of the woods yet. His situation could change for the better or for the worse. But we knew he was in God's hands, and God was in control.

They placed Chris in the trauma unit because he had severe, life-threatening injuries. The trauma floor required visitors to call and identify themselves. The staff identified us as his parents since Money and I were already at the hospital. Money was listed as his stepfather because I informed the staff that his biological father, Shawn, was on his way from Atlanta. All other visitors were required to identify themselves or be accompanied by us to see him.

The police told us not to discuss what happened to Chris in the waiting area. There was concern the shooter or anyone related to the incident might try to obtain details about Chris' condition. Yes, it was that serious. The police believed the shooting was gang related. My son didn't affiliate with gangs, but the police thought his shooting could've been part of a gang initiation. This was because he was the only person walking down the street when the shooting happened. While his case was still open, the fewer people that knew about his condition, the better.

I was finally told by the waiting room receptionist that I could see my son. I nervously walked down the hall to Chris' room and was overcome with so many emotions. I was happy Chris survived two surgeries but feared what I would see once I walked into his room. I entered my son's hospital room, scared of what my reaction would be to his appearance. So, I closed my eyes and prayed to God for strength.

Once I opened my eyes, I couldn't believe what I saw. My

baby was on a ventilator. His head and eyes were swollen, and his head was twitching. I wanted to cry, but I didn't want Chris to hear me and know he was sick. I covered my mouth in case any sounds that were attached to my emotions tried to escape.

Internally, I repeated to myself, "Not right now, Shawn! **DO NOT CRY!** Be strong for Chris."

It broke my heart to see my son on a ventilator. I couldn't tell whether he was awake or not because his eyes were so swollen. I looked at him and doubted if he knew I was in the room or even awake.

I walked to his bed, looked at his face, and kissed his forehead. I noticed Chris' nose ring was gone.

I thought, "Chris didn't tell me he got rid of his nose ring. I didn't like it, anyway."

I chuckled to myself but then refocused on why I was looking at him in the first place.

I asked him, "Who did this to you?"

As the question left my lips, Chris continued to twitch. I continued to talk to him and purposely ignored his twitching or looking at the ventilator. I looked around the room, then back at Chris' face as I listened to the ventilator. I wondered if he could see the tears in my eyes and if he would make it out of this hospital room.

I took a deep breath and whispered to Chris, "I need you to fight for your life."

Chris just had to survive his wounds. I needed him here with me and his siblings. I needed him to aggravate me when he said something silly or asked me to help him with a last-minute request, like borrowing my car to go to the barbershop, McDonald's, or the mall—anything but seeing him like this. I needed him to honor my request.

I continued talking to Chris and said, "Please fight for Mama. Chris, the doctors told me the first twenty-four to forty-eight hours are crucial for you to survive your injuries. I am not leaving this hospital until you walk out. So, Mama needs you to fight for your life, OK? I will be here the day you walk out of this hospital. I am not leaving your side until you do, Chris. There is a chair right next to your bed, and I am going to sit in the chair until you wake up. When you wake up, you will see me. OK? Son, please, fight! Please, I am staying right here by your side."

I couldn't talk anymore after that. I looked at him, held his hand, and kissed his forehead. I stared at him a bit, watching his head twitch. I finally sat in the chair by his bed and watched him twitch until it finally subsided. I continued to pray to God for Chris to make it through the night.

I had never felt so helpless in my life as I sat in the chair, watching and hearing the ventilator breathe for my son.

I looked at Chris and sadly asked again, "Who did this to you?"

Chapter 4
Wait, How Many Times?

While I sat with Chris, Money looked online for hotels close to the hospital for us to stay for the weekend or longer. We still didn't know how long we would stay in Columbia. At least, I was unsure. To me, it didn't matter how long. I wasn't leaving my son. At that moment, my job didn't matter. Nothing mattered. The only thing I cared about was Chris. I wanted my face to be the first thing he saw should he wake up from being heavily sedated.

The image of a ventilator breathing for my son, his head swollen and twitching, was hard for me.

As this image burned in my memory, Money said, "I found a hotel down the street from the hospital. It looks like a nice hotel."

He booked a room for us at the Holiday Inn Express and Suites.

Instantly, my body recalled that I hadn't slept for 24 hours. No sleep! I could feel my body about to crash and burn after being up for so long. My nerves and body were on edge, dealing with sleep deprivation. I felt overwhelmed. I had no control over what was going on around me. I was diagnosed with high blood pressure four years prior. When stressed, my

BP elevates to unsafe levels. I had to make sure my stress level stayed low, or I would be in the same hospital as my son.

There wasn't anything for us to do at this point, but wait. So, we figured this would be a good time to head to the hotel to freshen up and get some rest. The nurse asked for my phone number in case anything happened while we were gone.

She said, "I promise we will call if anything changes. Chris is in good hands, and you need rest. Ms. Wright, please take care of yourself because Chris needs you. If you do not take care of yourself, you won't be any good to your son."

I thought, "How do I get rest when my nerves are on edge?"

When Money and I got to our hotel room, we took our showers. After my head hit the pillow, I don't remember anything. I don't know how long I slept. Once I awoke and looked around, I realized we were not home on Pawleys Island.

My mind panicked, "Oh my God! We're in Columbia at a hotel by the hospital, and Chris is on a ventilator, fighting for his life. He was shot three times!"

I felt like I was in a daze as I remembered why I was there, and my heart sank. I was living a nightmare! I felt tears rolling down my cheeks. I prayed for God to give me strength as the images of Chris' head twitching and my conversation with his doctor on his chances of survival began to roll through my mind. His survival rate seemed very minimal, and I felt helpless. I had no control over this situation at all, which was the worst kind of feeling!

Money realized I was awake and asked if I wanted to go downstairs for the hotel's continental breakfast. At that moment, I realized I was just as hungry as I was tired and drained. I couldn't remember the last time I ate food. My stomach felt like it was in knots as I got dressed to go downstairs.

We left the room and took the elevator down to the hotel cafeteria. There were various small groups of people eating throughout. Money and I took our time as we looked over the buffet and made our plates. I found a table and sat down while Money continued to make his way around the buffet. As I turned and looked at the TV, the news anchor started reporting on the shooting of a twenty-three-year-old man on Tree Street near Millwood Avenue and Gervais Street.

The news anchor said, "The young man is in the hospital with serious injuries. If anyone has information on the shooting, please call Crime Stoppers."

All of the alarms sounded in my mind, "Oh My God, OH MY GOD, OH MY GOD! He just reported the shooting! Chris, he reported about Chris!"

Money came to the table in the middle of the news segment.

I looked at him and said, "He's talking about Chris!"

Money looked at me, then turned to look at the TV. What were the odds of us sitting at a table and hearing a news report about my son being shot? I sat at the table numb as I ate my breakfast, which now tasted like air. I no longer had an appetite. However, I needed to put nourishment in my body. We ate in silence as I tried to brace myself to return to the hospital. I didn't want to hear any more bad news about Chris. Truthfully, I wasn't sure if Money said anything to me or not because I mentally tuned out everything after the news report.

All I kept hearing was, "A twenty-three-year-old man was shot on Tree Street! He's in the hospital with serious injuries!"

As many times as Chris was shot, it should have killed him. It appeared that the shooter intended to kill, not maim. How could anyone survive multiple gunshot wounds when some people don't even survive one? The first twenty-four to forty-eight hours were crucial to Chris' survival. That's all I thought about as my mind replayed every detail.

After breakfast, Money and I got dressed to return to the hospital. Chris underwent two surgeries on the first day, so we were unsure how long he would remain on a ventilator. I tried to comprehend all that had happened—the shooting, the surgeries, and my son on a ventilator. His body had endured so much trauma. He needed to remain heavily sedated to prepare his body for the additional surgeries to repair the holes in his intestines. One hole had already been successfully closed, so he had four more to go. Deep in my soul, I didn't feel my son would die from his injuries or surgeries. I felt God's presence, believed He heard my prayers, and that He would heal my son.

We walked into Chris' room to the sight and sound of the ventilator breathing for him. It was a cruel reminder of his condition. I smiled as I looked him over and noticed the swelling in his face had gone down tremendously. I kissed his forehead, held his hand, and looked over his body. I was relieved because he looked like my son again, minus the ventilator.

There were pillows under his arms and restraints on his wrists in case he woke up and tried to take the tubes out. There was a bandage on his right leg, and both legs were wrapped to help circulate blood. Under the hospital gown, his stomach was open and covered with mesh since he still needed more surgeries to repair his intestines. I looked at Chris with sadness, but I was still filled with hope for his survival.

I quietly talked to Chris while Money sat in the chair near the bed. One of the nurses on duty walked into the room and introduced herself. She was very nice.

She asked, "Are you his mother?"

I replied, "Yes, and this is his stepfather. How's Chris doing today?"

She said, "He's doing as expected and still has a long road to recovery."

The nurse began to show us his various injuries, and I

became skeptical. My mind began to replay everything we were told since the beginning of this ordeal. First, we were told that Chris was shot in the leg. Then Mr. Johnson, the hospital liaison, told us Chris had been shot three times. However, the nurse pointed out more than three injuries.

First, she revealed the shot in his right leg and the exit wound. The wound was still open, and the sight of it almost caused me to vomit. The second wound was on his knee. The third wound was found under his left buttock. Then, the remaining wounds were the five holes in his intestines. We were perplexed when she explained all of this to us, which showed on our faces.

I spoke up and said, "We were told he was shot three times. You are showing us more wounds. So how many times was my son actually shot?"

The nurse looked at his records and replied, "Chris was shot eight times."

Confused, I asked, "Eight times? Do you mean four entrance and four exit wounds?"

She said, "No. Eight entrances and eight exits. Whoever shot your son emptied the gun to kill him."

Every hair on my body stood up as I looked at Chris. It hit me that my son was fighting for his life because he was shot in cold blood by someone he didn't know! The silence was deafening, leaving only the sound of the ventilator to fill the room.

I tried to keep my emotions in check and make sense of it all. I believed Chris could feel my energy, and I didn't want to give him any negativity. I needed positive energy around him so he could survive. But the notion of someone shooting my son so many times angered me. How dare this person do this to him? I was so angry and full of rage. But I had to put those emotions aside and focus only on Chris. He needed positive energy to heal. That's what I believed, and I stuck to it the entire time we were there.

I looked at Money and could see the shock on his face from what we'd just heard. He couldn't say a word. He just stared at Chris with his cell phone in hand, like he was scared to move in the moment. Once the shock wore off, Money and I looked at each other.

I said, "Eight times. Chris was shot eight times!"

I had so many unanswered questions that ran through my mind, but I knew I wouldn't obtain the answers yet. We watched the nurse check Chris' vitals and exit the room, which left us alone with Chris to process the nurse's words. After a brief time, I called my mother and sister to update them on Chris.

Shawn arrived from Atlanta sometime during the afternoon. He said he would sit with Chris until visiting hours were over. However, once he got in the room and saw Chris, he sat by his bed and didn't leave his son's side.

Money and I had been at the hospital most of the day. I was still tired from being up for 24 hours the day before. So, we told Shawn we were going back to the hotel to get some rest. Before we left the room, I watched Shawn sit back in the chair next to Chris, hold his hand, and almost immediately fall asleep.

I knew what happened to Chris took a toll on Shawn. Shawn loved his kids, especially Chris, because he was our oldest. Over the years, Shawn and I co-parented and became friends. We went through some things while raising our son, both as parents and as individuals. Chris was a good kid and went through typical growing pains. One thing was for certain: Chris had the love of both his parents, and we were not leaving his side. Whenever he woke up, he would see either me, Shawn, or both of us. We would get through this together as a family.

Once Money and I were in our hotel room, Money turned on the TV so we could decompress a bit. I looked at the text messages on my cell phone. There were so many messages from family and friends as they heard what happened to Chris. They wanted to check on me and see if I was alright and if they could do anything to help. Some even offered to come to the hospital and sit with me for moral support. I tried to respond to the texts as best as possible but was extremely exhausted. I knew everyone had questions, but so did we. However, the questions we had at the moment were not as important as getting through this crisis as a family.

Money called his mother and his sister, Quonda, to give them an update, along with the newfound information from the nurse. As long as Money and I have been together, his family has shown love towards my kids and myself. I knew they were equally concerned about Chris. Money kept them informed daily, just as I did with my family. After answering as many texts as I could, and Money finished talking to his family, we got ready for bed.

My mind and body were exhausted. I was mentally and emotionally drained. As we laid in silence, I closed my eyes and internally prayed for God to continue to be with my son, cover him with His embrace, and heal him. Sleep started to take over. I felt God's arms embrace me as I fell into a deep sleep.

God whispered to my spirit, "Sleep, my child, as tomorrow will be a better day."

Chapter 5
Family

The vision of seeing Shawn hold Chris' hand the night before was embedded in my mind. I had a flashback to when Chris was a baby. At times, Mrs. Vanderhorst, Chris's paternal grandmother, would pick up Chris to spend weekends at her home, or I would bring him over. I watched Shawn hold Chris in his arms and play with him. I remember thinking how beautiful it was to see a father and son bonding. I believe Shawn now held Chris' hand for strength and silently prayed for Chris to survive.

I didn't know how long I would be at Palmetto Health with Chris. I had accumulated a lot of vacation and sick leave, but I was unclear how it applied in this situation. So, I decided to contact my friend Alfreda, who worked in the Human Resource Department at the college. She was the one person on my job I could trust during this crucial time.

I emailed her before we left the hotel. She replied quickly and explained I qualified for FMLA (Family Medical Leave Act). It provides employees with up to twelve weeks of annual unpaid, job-protected leave. It also ensures the employee's group health benefits are maintained throughout their leave of absence. She gave me instructions for Chris' doctors to complete the FMLA form and fax it back to her department. Alfreda ended her email by expressing we were in her prayers and to focus on my son.

I also called Chris' job to inform them what happened. They sent me FMLA forms to complete on his behalf since he could not do it himself. On our way out of the hotel, I stopped by the internet cafe to print the forms and take them to the hospital. Once I walked into Chris' room, Shawn prepared to leave so he could get some sleep. He went to check into the hotel with a plan to stay for two weeks.

Once settled, I presented the FMLA paperwork to Chris' doctors. His doctors filled out the documents, and I quickly faxed them to our employers. After I faxed the forms, I took the time to read the doctor's written comments regarding Chris' condition.

It stated, "Multiple gunshot wounds; hemorrhagic shock; internal iliac artery and vein injury, gastric perforation, small bowel perforations (x5), sigmoid perforation, acute respiratory failure, and the patient remains in Surgical Trauma ICU in guarded condition."

Reading this caused me to understand the seriousness of Chris' condition and that he could die. I felt numb and helpless but didn't share the severity of Chris' condition with anyone. It would be real if I uttered those words or even thought them. Seeing him on a ventilator was hard enough.

I listened as the machine breathed for him and watched his body for signs of progress. My eyes took in the whole room. I prayed the machine wouldn't make a long beep sound like you see on TV when a person dies. That outcome would tear my soul completely apart. I didn't want to experience the long beep. Never, ever!

Days after I sent in both of our FMLA forms, my employer approved medical leave for four months. My return date to work was scheduled for May 1st. I also contacted my instructor and graduate program advisor to inform them of my medical leave. They officially placed me on hiatus from grad school.

Chris' job also approved his leave, and his supervisor told me to let them know if I needed anything. I thought that was so nice of them.

He said, "On behalf of the entire company, we are praying for him. Let us know when he recovers and returns to Columbia, and we will place him back on the work schedule."

I was relieved because I could now focus totally on my son.

AVERY WAS APPROACHING his 4th year in the Navy when Chris was shot. The Navy granted Avery permission to come home for two weeks after the American Red Cross forwarded Chris' medical report. Avery called me, and I knew he was upset because I could hear it in his voice. He was trying to deal with the fact that his brother had been shot, and the report looked dire.

After our phone conversation, Avery booked the next available flight from San Diego, California, to Columbia, South Carolina. He shared what time his flight would arrive at Columbia Metropolitan Airport. Unfortunately, I was alone at the hospital, and no one was available to pick him up from the airport.

Avery said, "Don't worry, mom. I'll use my phone to schedule a ride-share from the airport to the hospital."

Once Avery arrived at the hospital, we sat in the waiting area while I gushed over how grown he looked. I hadn't seen him since the summer of 2015 because they had stationed him out to sea. I was so happy to see him but wished it were under different circumstances. His presence made me feel I could deal with all that was going on around me. I felt stronger and like I gained some control over the chaotic situation.

Avery gave me "the Avery look" as he mustered the strength to see his brother. Avery had a way of looking at you with an annoyed face without saying a word. I am pretty sure it's the same look I used to give the kids when their questions made little sense. However, Avery had it down to a science. The look was meant to be comical, but this time, it meant he was worried. After this ordeal, I understood every unspoken meaning behind his facial expression.

At the same moment, my Aunt Frances and Uncle JB arrived at the hospital to sit with us for a while. Avery had already walked to Chris' room. I told the receptionist I would take my aunt to the room and leave since Avery was with Chris. She told me that was fine and gave us access to the ICU area. I noticed Avery walking down the hall in our direction with tears running down his face. Alarmed, I stopped him as my Aunt Frances stood by me, and I asked him why he was crying and if he was ok.

He looked at me with tear-filled eyes as he asked, "Who did this to him, Mama?"

The hurt in Avery's voice almost broke me.

With a cracked voice, he shared, "As I walked into the room, I saw the ventilator. I held his hand and asked him, 'Who did this to you?' I felt the tears run down my face and quickly walked out of the room so he wouldn't hear me crying."

I hugged my son so tightly and consoled him, but I felt helpless because I couldn't take his pain away. My children are close, and it pained me greatly to see them hurting and questioning the uncertainty of Chris' survival. My aunt consoled him as well because she saw I was overcome with emotion at the sight of my youngest son's devastation. I remembered hearing my aunt's words at that moment but not hearing them at the same time.

My Aunt Frances' words felt soothing, like a song, and it calmed us both. Avery told me he would stay in the waiting area with Uncle JB in case any more relatives came to the hospital. He wanted to be there so our family could see one of us was available to talk with them. My Uncle JB visited with Chris after my aunt. It was hard for them, but after they saw him and prayed with us, I truly appreciated all they had done.

Later, in our hotel room, Avery told me the Navy granted him two weeks' leave. He explained the Navy wouldn't send him home for just any reason. If an immediate family member is on the verge of dying or has died, the sailors were granted funeral leave and given time to handle affairs while on leave before reporting back to base for duty. Avery didn't say Chris was on the verge of dying from his wounds. He never told me the information in Chris' medical report given by the American Red Cross, and I never asked. I understood what he meant, and we both knew Chris' prognosis looked very grim.

After our conversation, I said silently to God, "Thank you, God, for sending my son Avery home, as I needed him to be with me during this time. God, if it is your will, and I know You hear my cries, please don't let Avery see his brother die in the hospital. Based on my conversation with him, he was sent home for that reason. By Your grace, he is here to witness his brother survive his injuries and possibly walk out of this hospital. Please be with my son Chris and give him continued strength to fight for his life. I know I am asking the impossible, but with You, all things are possible, right? God, you are in control. My will is strong, but You are in control. Thank you for being with me, my kids, and my family, as this is a hard experience as a mother. Seeing my child fighting, literally fighting for his life, is very hard to bear as his mother, and I wish I could take it all away from him. I pray You will be with me, too, so I can be strong for him as he needs me to be. Thank you, God. I love you with all my heart. Amen."

The emotions from the day took my mind back in time. I reflected on the moment Shawn shared with me that he prayed for Chris while he packed for the trip to the hospital. As his parents, it was hard facing the possibility of our son perishing from his injuries. Shawn told me he felt numb, shocked, and devastated that a stranger shot our son like he was target practice. He was angry and questioned who shot his son and why. He had many questions and couldn't wait to talk to the doctors for answers.

More questions were brought to both our hearts each time we looked at our son on a ventilator. To me, the image of Chris being on a ventilator was final. The machine made me focus on how peaceful Chris looked. I watched the air pump in his body and only heard the machine. He didn't look like he was in any pain. His face was peaceful despite the tubes connected all over his body. I often questioned how my son could look so at peace after so much trauma. I honestly looked for signs of him being in pain. A grimace. A moan. Anything, but nothing. He looked so much at peace. It wasn't a pretty sight, and I didn't expect it to be. I can only imagine what the nurses and doctors saw when Chris was wheeled into the emergency room after being shot.

Never in my life had I dealt with something like this. It felt so final and extreme. I had never seen a person on a ventilator, except on TV shows or movies. To my knowledge, Chris had to be on a ventilator and sedated due to the magnitude of his injuries surgeries and to increase his chances of survival.

To prevent my mind from replaying the dire circumstances, I remembered how my son would dance to make me laugh. Chris was skinny and 6' 2", and I liked to watch Chris' long skinny legs dance. He would often stop in front of me and dance just to make me laugh, then continue to walk toward his room or the kitchen like he had done nothing. I continued to envision Chris dancing because I strongly believed he would walk out of the hospital. Once he recovered fully from his injuries, he would walk by me and dance again to make me laugh.

Chapter 6

The Waiting Room

During the first two weeks, Shawn and I took turns sitting with Chris, as we wanted to make sure he saw our faces whenever he woke up. When Money and I were at the hospital, sometimes he would sit in the waiting room to give me time alone with Chris. One day, Chris woke up while I sat in the chair beside his bed.

Oh my God, he was awake. He was awake! Thank you, Jesus! Chris had a puzzled look on his face as his eyes looked around the room. Then he looked down at his hands and saw his hands strapped to the bed. He realized there were tubes in his throat because he couldn't talk. So, I spoke to my son.

I said, "You've been admitted to the hospital because you were shot."

He shook his head, acknowledging what I said, but looked down at his hands, then back at me.

Then I said, "Yes, you are strapped to the bed."

He gave me the puzzled look again, like he was asking me, "Why?"

I said, "The reason you are strapped is so you won't get up."

Still confused by what I said, I proceeded to tell him what was told to me by the nurse, the doctor, and Mr. Johnson.

I explained, "When you were brought to the emergency room, they thought you had been shot in your leg. But doctors soon realized you were shot more than once. You were shot eight times, and so far, you've had two surgeries. You have five holes in your intestines. The doctor already closed one hole, but she felt you could die of septic shock if she closed all five holes at once. Right now, your stomach is open. Your intestines are covered by a mesh, and if you stand up, which I know you won't do, your intestines will fall on the floor. I need you to relax and not panic. Can you do that for Mama?"

It drained me to explain what had happened to Chris. I felt like I couldn't breathe. Chris had no clue what was going on around him, and I believed if I slowly explained the situation to him, he wouldn't panic. I kept my feelings in check as I shared his circumstances with him. It hurt me to my core as his mother not to inform him he was close to death. I could see Chris trying to grasp and comprehend every detail as I spoke. Then Chris slowly nodded his head "yes" and closed his eyes back into the induced coma, leaving me to hear only the ventilator.

I felt every part of my body ache as I looked at him while the machine pumped air into his skinny body. I could imagine the thoughts and questions in his head, like how one bullet could do all this. His intestines were out, his legs wrapped in gauze, something else stimulating his legs to keep the blood from clotting, and he was on a ventilator fighting for his life!

At that moment, I didn't know if he understood all that happened to him. His body had endured both surgeries and injuries that could have killed him. I really didn't think the doctors expected him to survive. Every time I spoke with a different doctor, each one told me they were fighting to save his life. As encouraging as those words were, the compassion I felt from the doctors made me feel they cared, even though the situation was dire.

After Chris went back into sedation, Chris' doctors requested we let his body rest for a day. Then, they scheduled the surgery to close the second hole in his intestines. After that, Money and I left the hospital for the day, while Shawn remained a little longer before he retired for the night.

OUR FAMILIES WERE CONCERNED for Shawn and I, as well as Chris. As I stated before, both of us came from large families. Shawn was the youngest of nine children. I am the oldest of three, not including my stepfather's seven children. Once our siblings, uncles, aunts, and cousins heard what happened to Chris, they called and made plans to visit the hospital and surround us with moral support.

The support from my siblings and both sides of the family meant so much to me. We needed it more than ever to help us get through this crisis. It was still early, and the outcome could go either way. Chris was not out of the woods yet, as there were multiple surgeries coming up.

Dawn stayed with my daughter, Bri, until Money returned home to Pawleys Island. Then Dawn came to sit with me at the hospital. Our brother, Brucie, still served in the National Guard at the time, so he was unable to get away, but Dawn gave him daily reports on Chris' prognosis. I commissioned her as the designated person to report news and updates to both sides of the family, so my focus could remain on Chris and his recovery.

My great-aunt Audrey called and sent prayers, as well as others who were unable to visit the hospital, to let us know they were thinking of us. I understood because I would never ask my family or anyone to stop their lives to come to the hospital. Even though I welcomed the support, it felt selfish to ask that of them. I valued and appreciated every inquiry and visit, as I felt their genuine concern. At the time, we had everything under control. If Chris' condition turned for the worse, our families would swiftly be notified.

My stepfather, Willie, was bedridden, and my mother was his caregiver because he needed around-the-clock care. When she was able to arrange coverage, she rode to the hospital with my Aunt Debbie. My Aunt Debbie had always felt a closeness to Chris since he was a baby. She and my mother helped me the first three months after Chris was born, so they both wanted to be there for me and Chris. When Shawn and I would switch shifts from sitting with Chris, we called our kids and families and gave them updates. We tried to communicate with our families as best we could, and I think we did a good job based on the circumstances. Our families didn't know, but they gave us the strength to endure this ordeal.

When our family would visit, we all sat in the waiting room because Chris was only allowed two visitors at a time. Every family member who wanted to see Chris would wait patiently for Shawn or myself to escort them to his room. As we walked our family members to his bedside, we requested that they not cry while with him because Chris could sense their energy.

I noticed how Chris responded to my energy when I was with him. When Chris heard my voice, he sometimes rubbed my hand or opened his eyes and looked in my direction. I spoke to him in a loving way, and he acknowledged my words by nodding his head before he returned to a heavily sedated coma. I only wanted positive energy in the room to help motivate him to fight for his life. I felt it wasn't good for his survival if everyone cried while in his presence. In my opinion, crying told Chris he wasn't going to survive and would die from his injuries. I didn't want that for my son. He needed to fight.

Regardless of how dire the situation may have looked, I wanted positive energy from everyone.

To my surprise, everyone respected our request to leave his presence if they felt emotional and needed to cry. They collected themselves in the hallway or bathroom, then went back in if they wanted to continue to sit with him. Otherwise, I walked them back to the waiting room with the other family members and friends. I was thankful no one objected or counteracted my wishes.

Our families mostly visited on the weekends and arrived at different times. If Shawn was in Chris' room, I stayed in the waiting room talking to family members.

As I sat there, I often heard the elevator door open, followed by the familiar greeting, "Hey, Shawn."

Both sides of our families reeled from what happened to Chris. Hence, they arrived at the hospital with a lot of questions. We had so many visitors the first two weeks Chris was in the hospital. We welcomed their support and presence because it diverted us from worrying about our son.

There were laughable moments as I sat in the waiting room with my family members. One day, my Uncle Jackie and his friend, Denise, badgered back and forth with one another. I was shocked by their interaction, and they made me laugh so much that I cried tears of joy. Shawn's oldest brother, Glennis, also made me laugh during his visit to the hospital. His great sense of humor helped me not to worry so much about Chris.

Chris' first visitors were his friends, Darius and Brian, aka Rico. I could tell they were hurt and deeply concerned when they saw me. I updated them on his condition and the chances of his survival. They tried to contain their emotions and comprehend all I shared with them. Darius took it the hardest because he and Chris were roommates and a big part of each other's lives.

It felt like I had a shield covering my emotions as I refused to allow people to see me cry. I focused on everyone else rather than myself to help me combat any negative thoughts and fears. In my mind, my son would not succumb to his injuries. I believed I could help guide him through the healing process as long as I maintained this belief.

My tears remained bottled up until I was alone in my hotel room. Then, I would release and cry until I couldn't cry anymore. Afterward, I talked to God because only He understood how I felt and could guide me through this ordeal.

I told the hospital receptionist I gave Darius and Brian permission to visit Chris together, as they were his best friends. She allowed it, but before they walked to Chris' room, I shared my stance on crying in his room.

I said, "Please try not to cry because he will sense something is wrong, and I don't want him thinking that."

They nodded in agreement and replied, "OK, Ms. Shawn."

I smiled at Chris' friends for encouragement as the receptionist buzzed them in the door. As Darius and Brian walked towards the door, I breathed deep and said a silent prayer before I sat back down in the waiting room chair. I stared at the TV on the wall but couldn't focus on what was playing on the screen. I felt numb, and the TV was my only diversion until someone I knew stepped out of the elevator.

I sat there, willing the elevator door to open, just to see a familiar face emerge. I felt if I thought about what happened to my son, I would be overwhelmed with sadness. I couldn't do that to myself or my son. My son needed me, and that affirmation remained my focus the whole time I sat in the waiting room.

It seemed like Darius and Brian stayed with Chris forever. They came back and shared how emotional the visit made them. Although I had warned them before going back, nothing could've really prepared them for what they would see. From Chris' appearance to the ventilator, they tried to comprehend all that had happened to their friend. They were full of questions and mortified by what happened to Chris and the thought that it could happen to them.

Chris wasn't just their friend. He was their brother. Thinking back on the boys' friendship with Chris, their brotherhood started when they were little boys in elementary school. They played recreational basketball together and then went on to play together in middle and high school. When Chris transferred to Waccamaw High School's team, I was concerned about their friendship continuing since they would now be opponents rather than teammates. However, their friendship never diminished and is one to be admired and commended.

Darius and Rico talked to Chris while they were in his room, and he slowly responded to their voices despite being sedated. The doctor, who was also in the room, noted that was progress because Chris hadn't shown much activity since being admitted. Although they were happy to hear this bit of news, their emotions quickly changed back to hurt. They had to watch their best friend and brother lay in a hospital bed on a ventilator, eyes closed, unable to talk, and in a sedated state.

After visiting with Chris, Darius and Rico shared that Chris had moved his hands. They were happy and saw it as a sign. I could see the sadness on their faces as they told me they would return once they checked their work schedules. The boys had lives of their own, and I didn't expect them to stop everything to sit with me at the hospital. I knew when given a chance, they would visit and help as much as they could.

I gave both boys a tight hug and said, "Thank you for coming."

They replied, "We had to come so Chris knows we're here for him. We promise we'll be back soon."

True to their word, the boys encouraged their other friends to visit Chris. Jasmar came a few days later, and his demeanor was sad as he walked into Chris' room. However, he returned to the waiting area an hour later, smiling and laughing.

Jasmar said, "Ms. Shawn, Dub is going to be alright! Dub saw me and tried to communicate. He tried to get out of his bed."

He laughed, and it was so joyous to hear laughter, something I hadn't heard since I arrived at the hospital. It was music to my ears after and gave me hope. To hear Jasmar tell me he believed Chris would be alright left me ecstatic. It was the best news at that time, and I wanted to cry tears of joy. All my ears heard were doctors and nurses talking to me about my son in medical terms I didn't understand, which left me asking for meaning or clarity.

The TV and ventilator were the only sounds I heard when I was alone in Chris' room. I would listen to the ventilator with a blank look on my face and pray my son wouldn't flatline. My cell phone became my diversion, and I welcomed access to the outside world. I continuously received text messages from friends and family members who sent words of encouragement and prayers.

A couple of days after Chris was admitted, another of his best friends, Datron, aka Dada, contacted me through Facebook Messenger. He had heard about Chris and wanted us to know he and his family were praying for us all. Datron and Chris had been friends since middle school and grew up in the same apartment community. They also kept in touch with each other after graduation. I told Datron the details of the shooting, Chris' prognosis, and how he was fighting for his life.

Shawn sat with Chris in the room and told him his friend, Datron, was coming to see him. Shawn texted me and said Chris nodded in response to Datron's message. When Datron and his wife Emily visited Chris, I knew he was happy to see them. Even though Chris was in and out of heavy sedation, hearing his friend's voice was enough. Datron messaged me daily for updates on Chris' progress after his visit.

My cousins, Siobhan and Missy, came from North Carolina and offered their love and support for Chris as soon as they arrived. I sat down with them in the waiting room. They listened intently as I shared the latest update on him. They, too, were allowed to go in together while I stayed behind in the waiting room. The receptionist buzzed Siobhan and Missy into the ICU, and they were on their way.

For my relatives, the walk to Chris' room seemed like a long journey to the unexpected. Imagine walking a long corridor to a room where you are unsure of what to expect. Let alone how you will react to what you see once there. The anxiety and anticipation get the best of you. Even though you were told what to expect, seeing it with your own eyes was different.

My cousins shared how they walked into Chris' room and were stunned as their hearts dropped. Anger crept into their souls as they watched their younger cousin breathe with the help of a machine. The more they listened to the ventilator, the angrier they became. Like me, they had questions. Who did this to their cousin, and why? What motive did this person or people have to shoot him down like an animal? All sorts of questions were in their minds, but they kept their composure, walked into his room, and honored my requests.

From their account, it was the hardest thing for them to do, but they inched closer towards Chris' bed. Siobhan touched his hand and prayed for him to be OK. She needed God to heal him. He didn't move as they looked down at him. Seeing Chris like this felt like the worst day of their lives. As Missy talked to Chris, his eyes didn't open, but he did move his hands in response. Siobhan touched and held his hand, and he moved his hand to touch hers. It was a sign to them he would survive. It was an emotional yet amazing visit, as they experienced Chris respond to their presence through touch.

My cousins weren't the only ones who experienced this. The surprise touch of Chris' hands and his eyes opening briefly were his way of communicating with us. We were mindful to leave a relative in the room with him in case he woke up again or touched their hands. These basic actions were like a sign from God he would survive his injuries. It was the sweetest thing to see and hear each person share what they experienced during their visit with Chris.

By now, the receptionist knew me on a first name basis as I rarely left the hospital. I was there throughout her shift and beyond. I only went to the hotel to sleep for a couple of hours while Shawn was in Chris' room. Then, I would return so Shawn could sleep for a couple of hours. Shawn and I ensured we got some form of rest and diversion from the hospital. Even if it meant we stood outside and looked at the trees for a couple of hours, we needed some sort of peace and calm amid the chaos.

When I was alone in my hotel room, I could still faintly hear the ventilator in my mind. I welcomed any diversion around me that brought calm, solitude, and, above all, privacy. I talked so much each day that I welcomed the brief opportunity not to speak with anyone about Chris.

It really touched me when Dawn came to see him. She was so much help to me from the start. She ensured my daughter had a little normalcy while I was away. She even cleaned my house, so when Bri and Money came home, they didn't have anything to do. Money worked during the week and came to the hospital on weekends so he could be there with me at the hospital.

When Dawn was able, she came to the hospital, sat with me, made me laugh, and helped out as much as possible. On her first visit, she reluctantly walked into Chris' room. She shared the same apprehension and anxiety as everyone else who would see him for the first time. She spoke to the nurse and sat down in the chair next to Chris' bed. She reached for his hand and rubbed his hand as she talked to him. She was shocked when he rubbed her hand back.

My sister was so happy, she recorded it on her phone. She finished talking to him, kissed his forehead, and quickly walked down the hall to the waiting room. She was so happy as she sat down next to me.

She said, "Look at this," and showed me the video of her holding his hand and Chris rubbing her hand back.

When Dawn realized what he was doing, she stopped, but he continued to rub her hand. She was so shocked because she didn't expect him to react to her presence. He was sedated but still unconsciously heard her voice. Tears filled my eyes as I watched the video. It was such an emotional moment for me and the sweetest gesture from him.

I believe Chris was telling me, "See, Mama, I'm still fighting!"

I gave my sister permission to share the video on her social media page. Even now, when the video memory appears in my feed, I watch it and get teary-eyed. It's one of those cherished moments for me as I recall that day, how I felt, and the chaos of this journey. I felt joy seeing Chris rub Dawn's hands, and I still envision him doing so. It was a beautiful, precious moment eclipsed in time for me to remember forever.

CHRIS' cousins on both sides of the family inquired in the streets about what happened in Columbia.

As they said, "People talk, but not always to the police. You just focus on Chris and his survival."

In other words, the less I knew, the better. It was laughable to me because they told me not to worry about how they would get the information. Unfortunately, the streets didn't talk to them either. What little they heard was thin since the incident was considered a random drive-by shooting.

A host of family members, colleagues, and friends, so many I can't name them all, stopped by to visit or pray for Chris and our family. Our family members on both sides and their church families prayed continually for Chris, which meant a lot to all of us. Chris was briefly awake when my nephew Christian and his father, Chris "CP," came to visit. Christian asked Chris if he could pray for him, and Chris nodded in agreement. Then, he went back to sleep after Christian's prayer. Chris and Christian always had a bond between them even though Chris was the oldest and Christian was the baby out of the five children between my twin sister and myself.

Then came the "come to Jesus" moment while Shawn's sister, Ruthanne, was visiting with us. While in the waiting room, the doctor came to inform us that Chris had a biliary obstruction and wasn't doing well. While the doctor spoke with us, she made Chris's survival seem very grave. This was one of those times I seriously thought it was time to contact the funeral home. With no empathy in her voice, the doctor spewed a bunch of medical terms at us.

Then she looked at us and said, "Your son may not survive. Do you have any questions?"

I stood in pure shock at her lack of compassion.

Shawn looked at me and asked, "Do you have any questions?"

I looked at him with a blank look on my face, then sternly replied in her direction, "No, I do not!"

Shawn thanked the doctor for giving us the update. After she left, I cried. Shawn looked at me. I knew he wanted to cry as well, but he held it in.

Shawn told me he was going outside and assured me that Chris would be fine. Internally, I'm sure he tried to make sense of what the doctor told us. I feared he was also starting to believe Chris may not be okay after all.

Before going outside, Shawn walked over to Ruthanne and shared the doctor's news. She quickly got up, walked over, and hugged me.

She said, "God is in control, and the doctor only did what she was trained to do. There is no need to worry about Chris because he is in God's hands. You have to stay strong for Chris. He needs both of his parents' strength."

I listened intently to Ruthanne's words and stopped crying as Shawn, still reeling from the news, walked to the elevator.

I kept my best friends updated on Chris' condition as much as I could. They often texted me that they were praying for us all. They knew I was preoccupied at the hospital. However, whenever I got a moment to read their messages, I would gain strength from their encouraging words.

Later that day, while sitting in the waiting area, Tee, Chris' first cousin, tried to persuade me to eat dinner while her brother, Jamal, sat with Chris. I told Tee multiple times I didn't have an appetite.

She replied, "Auntie, you need to eat something."

Eventually, she decided to leave to pick up food for herself.

As she walked away, she said, "Whether you want it or not, I'm bringing you something back too."

Meanwhile, my good friend Elanda texted to ask for the hospital address. I sent her the information.

Then she asked, "Did you receive the flowers I sent?"

I replied, "No, not yet."

She proceeded to ask additional questions, and I wondered why she was suddenly texting me so many questions. I heard the elevator door open as another message came in from Elanda, but I didn't look in that direction.

Confused, I read the text aloud and said, "Shawn, look up?"

I looked up, and Elanda and Kena were standing in front of me. I laughed so hard at the excitement of seeing them. As we hugged, I began to cry because I remembered why we were all there. Once I regained my composure, we sat down and shared the latest updates on Chris.

To create a diversion from the grim news, they shared how their trip to Columbia came about. With plans to surprise me, they drove straight from work. They both had different versions of the same story. But in Kena's version, Elanda bullied her the entire drive to Columbia. I must admit that Kena's taped-up glasses made her version even more believable. Of course, all this was said to make me laugh.

Like Tee, they asked if I had eaten and fussed at me when I told them I had not. I don't eat when I am stressed. However, I didn't want to get sick from malnourishment. They stayed with me a bit before leaving to check in at the hotel, as they were tired from work and the drive to Columbia. They promised to return in the morning and take me to breakfast to ensure I ate something. Their presence alone made a world of difference to me.

Every interaction our family and friends had with Chris that showed signs of life encouraged me and gave me hope during this crisis. When speaking of his condition, I resolved to use the phrase "heavily sedated" because, to me, the word coma sounded dire and dreadful.

During the weekdays at the hospital, it was mainly Shawn and I and sometimes Money. Our families would pack out the waiting area on the weekends. Dawn faithfully updated my mother and family members since each day was a different status report on Chris. The doctors continued to operate on Chris, closing the holes in his intestines until the final surgery, removing the bullet in his right knee. The bullet wasn't as life threatening as the holes in his intestines. Surgery was scheduled for every other day, and no visitors were permitted on surgery days to allow Chris' body to recover from each procedure.

It was easy to sit in the waiting room and talk with family and friends about what happened to Chris and his progress. However, the receptionist pulled us aside one day with an important reminder.

She said, "Do not talk too much about your son or what happened. Remember, whoever shot Chris could be sitting in the waiting room and listening to his prognosis."

It was something we had been told initially, but it easily slipped our minds as we sat with concerned loved ones traveling from all over to support us. Since Chris' case was still under investigation, we all needed to be mindful of what we discussed. We did not know if they would try to retaliate against Chris because he showed signs of survival.

Whoever shot him may want him dead. The receptionist's words gave me an eerie feeling as I looked around the room. There were plenty of other people sitting in the waiting area to see their loved ones, too. I had to pay close attention to everyone sitting in the waiting room with me and my family. That was the last thing I needed–to have to look at every stranger with suspicion instead of solely focusing on my son's survival.

Chapter 7

February Miracle

Chris had endured five surgeries in over a week's time. The last surgery removed the bullet from the back of his right knee and closed the last hole in his intestines. Five days after Chris' last surgery, the doctors felt his body was strong enough to be removed from the ventilator. This was a relief to us because it meant his fragile body could finally breathe on its own.

I worried every time my son returned to the operating table because every surgery was life threatening. I never stopped praying because his condition was so delicate. Prayer was always constant in my life, but it took on a greater significance during this situation. I talked to God each time I learned something new about Chris' condition. I knew my relationship with God was personal, as I felt His presence with us every day.

To help Chris recover, the doctors decided only to allow the immediate family to visit him during the week. I appreciated their decision because it gave me alone time with him. I could now watch him sleep without seeing multiple tubes in his body or hearing the ventilator. The single tube in his nose was all that remained and was proof of Chris' progress. Even though the odds were against him, my son survived.

Shawn, Avery and I still took turns sitting with Chris, so whenever he woke up, one of us was in the room. I felt better knowing we were all there in case anything happened, good or bad. I stayed in the room as much as possible because I needed to hear Chris breathe, and he needed to know I was there for him, no matter what.

Shawn had plenty of questions about his son's condition for the doctors and nurses. I believe he asked almost a thousand well-thought-out questions, and they patiently answered everyone. I think he even looked up things to ask on his phone in addition to the questions he already had in his head. Shawn had an inquisitive mind, and if he wanted to know what was going on with his son, he was going to ask. I would not have thought about some of the questions Shawn asked. He wanted us both to know everything about our son.

The nurses and doctors noticed the difference between us. Shawn asked a list of questions and relayed everything he learned to me. However, I only sat in the room, smiled and greeted the nurses when they came in, watched Chris like a hawk, and cared for his needs.

Each time the nurses walked in and administered medication to Chris, Shawn, and I asked for the specific details of each drug. Do I remember what they told us? No, but I was just thankful the medication was helping him to recover. We were grateful for the medications they gave Chris during the surgeries and the recovery period. I believe every dose contributed to his chances of survival. We were also thankful for the hundreds of transfusions and platelets. For the first couple of surgeries, I pleaded with God not to let Chris die from the excessive blood loss he suffered. Deep down, I was fearful. However, I had no control over this ordeal, so I relied on God because He did.

During Chris' time in the hospital, the nurses saw me as a

fixture in the unit because I was with Chris all day, every day. They wondered if I ever went home. If I had my way, I would have slept in a chair next to his bed, but there was no space in the trauma unit to lie down. There was only an uncomfortable chair. I informed the nurses that I wasn't from the area and was staying at a nearby hotel. It was two hours each way to drive from my home on the island to the hospital in Columbia, which left the hotel as my only option.

My hotel stay wasn't cheap, so my work colleagues graciously raised money to help pay for the first two weeks. Our friends who visited us also brought greeting cards with money inside. It blessed me to apply the funds to my hotel fees. I budgeted my stay in Columbia very well and saved on my expenses.

Money returned to Pawleys Island after all of Chris' surgeries were complete, so I gave him updates on Chris by phone. I established a daily routine—pray before I get out of bed in the morning, turn on the TV while I shower, and get dressed to go to the hospital. The TV was my constant companion since I was in the hotel room by myself with no one to talk to. I was on a budget, so I didn't eat out at restaurants. Wal-Mart was within walking distance from the hotel, but with what happened to my son, I knew better than to walk in Columbia.

Each day, as I drove to the hospital, it gave me anxiety to see people walking around outside. I would pray that what happened to Chris didn't happen to them. After I visited with Chris on Sundays, I shopped at Wal-Mart and bought my food for the week. My groceries consisted of oatmeal, coffee, creamer, plastic utensils, healthy dinners, and snacks. Most of the time, the items I purchased from Wal-Mart would last about two weeks.

I went to the hospital cafeteria for lunch while Chris slept, which gave me the opportunity to leave his room for at least 30 to 40 minutes. It was a break from hearing machines, watching Chris sleep, and seeing the nurses come and go out of his room. I tried to eat a healthy lunch to maintain my strength. Before I left Chris' room, I would turn the TV channel back to ESPN. This way, if he woke up while I was away, he wouldn't know that I had changed the channel while he was asleep.

Sitting in the cafeteria restored some normalcy to my life. It allowed me to interact with people when I ordered food or stood in line at the register. I ate my lunch alone while I took in all the sounds around me. It was a welcomed diversion from what was happening upstairs in the trauma unit.

Once I finished lunch, I took the elevator right back to Chris' room. When I walked in, he would still be asleep or awake watching ESPN or something else on TV. I left daily for the hotel around seven or eight o'clock and felt funny walking into a dark hotel room. Sometimes, if I had extra money, I stopped at a nearby Chinese restaurant and bought wonton soup. My mother always said that soup was good for the soul. I felt the wonton soup was good for my soul, and it became a comfort food to calm my emotions. I was soon a regular face at the restaurant.

The server would ask, "wonton soup, right?"

And I would reply with a smile, "Yes, ma'am."

I would pay for my order, drive back to the hotel, and watch TV in my room while I ate my soup. I took a shower and got ready for bed once I finished dinner. Before I retired for the night, I called my mother and sister and gave them updates on Chris. Then, I slept my weary day away. Each morning, I started my routine over until Chris was eventually discharged weeks later.

One day, I was stopped by one of the trauma unit nurses in the hallway as I walked toward Chris' room. She commended me for visiting my man and noticed my commitment to come every day. Internally, I questioned why she was referring to Chris as my man.

Perplexed, I looked at the nurse and asked, "How old do you think I am?"

At the time, I had my hair in long locs, and gray hair had begun to show from worry, anxiety, and stress.

She replied, "You are in your 30s."

I said, "No, ma'am! I'm 46 years old, and the man you commend me for seeing is my oldest son, who is 23 years old. I have two other children as well."

The nurse looked at me in shock as though she didn't believe me. Apparently, I looked really young to her and the other nurses in the trauma unit. I laughed so hard in response to her shocked face. Then, I got serious and shared Chris' unfortunate story with the nurse.

She looked at me in amazement and said, "You don't show any signs of stress based on what happened."

She looked toward Chris' room and back at me.

With empathy, she continued, "May God continue to keep him and you."

I thanked her and proceeded to walk into Chris' room. I chuckled. I thought it was funny how they assumed Chris was my boyfriend and not my son. The same occurrence happened years prior at a shopping mall in Myrtle Beach. I took Chris clothes shopping before the start of his freshman year at Georgetown High School. We walked to the register, and I noticed the cashier wore a Georgetown High sweatshirt.

I asked, "Are you a student at Georgetown High?"

She replied, "Yes."

I then asked her, "What advice do you have for my son? He's a freshman."

She stared at us and asked, "He's your son? You're his mother?"

I laughed, but Chris had an annoyed look on his face.

I replied, "Yes, he's my oldest son."

She said, "Oh my God! You look too young to have a son going to high school."

I thanked her for the compliment as she proceeded to give him some advice about the high school.

As my sons became older, if a person heard them say, "Mama," people gave us shocked looks and commented how they couldn't believe my sons were my children. It was always hilarious to me but never to them, and both my sons were taller than me, which didn't help. So when the nurse approached me in the hospital, I thought about the past moments, chuckled, and was glad Chris didn't hear her call him "my man!"

꩜

CHRIS HAD difficulty speaking once they removed the ventilator from his throat. It left him with a continuously parched throat and hoarse voice. He constantly drank water and spit in a cup. The nurse provided a suction tube to help with the saliva that formed in his mouth. Hearing the suction noise and watching Chris spit disgusted me, even though I knew it was a struggle for him. I knew it irritated him to continually spit and place the suction tube in his mouth to remove the excess saliva. All in all, Chris was still happy the ventilator was out of his throat. The nurse told him he would feel better in a couple of days since he had been intubated for a week.

The incision on Chris' abdomen slowly closed over time. It was long and an inch or two wide. His flesh looked like a raw, bloody steak out of the package. At least, that's how it looked to me. Scary, indeed.

The time came for Chris to be weaned off the pain medication. I freaked out when Money and I walked into his room, and Chris was acting so erratically. He couldn't control his arms. They kept involuntarily going up and down.

When the nurse entered his room, I asked, "What's wrong with him?"

She explained, "The doctors are weaning him off the pain medication. So, his body is going through withdrawals. I know it looks bad, but he will be fine."

I stood beside Chris' bed, held his hand, and told him he would be fine. The only thing I knew to do was hold his hand and try to keep him calm.

Scared, Chris looked into my eyes and said, "Promise me, I won't stop breathing."

I turned my head and looked at Money with fear. His face mirrored the same fear. I looked back at Chris, nodded my head, and gave him a motherly smile.

I said, "I won't let you stop breathing. I promise. I won't let you do that."

The panic I saw on Chris' face was hard for me to deal with. I believed I would fail him if I couldn't calm him down and help control his experience. Failing him was not an option. So, I mustered the strength to guide him through the ordeal. I wanted to crawl into the bed with him to help him through it. He looked at me for guidance. Even though I was afraid, my son didn't see fear on my face. All Chris saw was strength as I guided him to a calm state.

He said, "Mama, don't leave me. I love you, Mama."

I replied, "I know I love you too, Chris."

To experience my son going through withdrawals from the medication was overwhelming. I never thought I would witness something so disturbing. What possibly took minutes felt like hours as I watched him have no control over his body. I looked at Money again as we both stood speechless by Chris' bed. I monitored every breath Chris took to maintain my promise to him.

I seriously wanted to cry from the unbearable pain and

trauma I felt as I watched Chris panic and plead to live. He was scared to death at the thought of not being able to breathe. He had no control over his body and looked at me for help. But there was no manual on how to help your son overcome life-threatening injuries. The only guidance I had was prayer.

When Chris finally fell asleep, I closed my eyes and prayed to God for strength as I fought back tears. I refused to cry. I felt crying was a sign of defeat and that I wasn't strong. I refused to let the devil win. So, I stood firm in my faith and focused my strength on guiding both myself and my son through this ordeal.

I looked over Chris' body as he now laid in a calm state. I noticed the doctors had installed what appeared to be a stoma near the incision on his abdomen. To me, the stoma resembled a large wad of chewed-up red gum stuck to the side of his stomach. Chris said it looked like a butt hole on the side of his stomach. Although the stoma looked like it hurt, Chris said it didn't.

I also observed that Chris had a colostomy pouch and a urinary catheter. I wondered how long he would have them and prayed it would be temporary and not permanent. As with everything else, their removal depended on his progress.

The nurse explained, "The laparotomy procedure will repair the damage to his large intestines, and the colostomy pouch allows his stool to bypass the damaged part of his colon. It is required until his intestines fully heal."

The pouch was attached to a barrier around his stoma, and the nurses replaced it daily. Chris felt all of it was an inconvenience, especially since he had no control over it. I must admit, I never saw or smelled poop in the pouch the entire time Chris was in the hospital because the nurses changed the bag often. Fortunately, I didn't have to deal with it until after Chris was discharged from the hospital.

I had no desire to be a nurse, but learning about laparotomy and colostomy somehow made me feel a little knowledgeable. I was curious to know how each treatment helped Chris progress and survive. I learned something new each time the nurses answered my questions. Every day, I watched the nurses empty the canister and place it back by the side of his bed. Occasionally, I emptied the canister so the nurses had one less thing to do for him. It gave me something to do besides sitting by his bed all day.

After noticing the little things I would do to help out with Chris, the nurses thought I was a nurse by trade.

Several nurses asked, "Are you a registered nurse?"

I always replied, "No, I'm just his mom."

I thanked every nurse who came in to check on Chris or administer his medication. I appreciated their commitment to my son's health. I observed everything they did for Chris and did my best to retain every detail. It was during this time I began to learn how to care for my son, unaware it was helping me prepare to step in as his caregiver.

One morning I arrived at the hospital and found the nurses had elevated Chris' bed. He could now sit up and watch ESPN rather than lie flat on his back. Chris and I had adopted a daily routine with the TV in his room. I would sit in his room and pretend to watch TV with him while I periodically responded to texts or calls on my cell phone. Once Chris went to sleep, I changed the TV channel to comedy shows, as I didn't want to watch the news. I welcomed anything that made me laugh and took my mind off of everything going on around me.

A couple of weeks had passed, and I was still wearing the clothes I brought with me when Chris was first admitted to the hospital in rotation. I didn't want to be away from Chris, but Shawn encouraged me to take a break.

He told me, "Go home and handle your business. Chris will be fine."

So, Avery and I drove home to Pawley's Island to wash

our clothes. Although it was for just one day, it felt funny leaving Chris for a whole day. However, I needed to wash clothes, check in with my daughter and Money, and pack more clothes. I also grabbed my electronic book reader from home so I could read while I sat with Chris.

Shawn stayed with Chris for the entire day while I was gone. After I returned to the hospital, Shawn began to prepare for his return to Atlanta. It was also time for Avery to report back to the Naval base in San Diego. For two weeks, Shawn and Avery were a constant at the hospital with me and witnessed each of Chris' milestones.

Avery witnessed one of the first major milestones when Chris walked for the first time on February 3, 2017. That day, Avery sat with Chris while I hung out in the waiting area. Avery came into the waiting room with a big smile on his face.

He exclaimed, "Mama, Chris walked today! Nurse Karen helped Chris walk with a walker.

Nurse Karen told Chris, 'I know you're tired of being in bed. Let's walk a little bit.'

Then she had me help her get him out of the bed, and he walked down the hall a short way with his walker."

It was such an exciting time. After all Chris had been through, it didn't matter who saw Chris take his first steps. The miracle was that my son walked! He had the strength given by God to get out of bed and literally take his first steps toward a full recovery. I was so happy. It was the best news so far in his amazing progress.

I said a silent prayer of thanks to God for the miracle and tried not to cry. This was a beautiful gift from God, and I was grateful for His presence. This journey was overwhelming, scary, and stressful, but at that moment, I felt pure joy and happiness. It was like I had just received both a Christmas and birthday gift at the same time. I was so excited I wanted to do cartwheels and a split! In spite of all my son went through, he walked.

I decided I had to share this miracle moment with the world. I love history and, before the shooting, would regularly share social media posts for Black History Month. However, since the shooting, I hadn't been in the mood to post facts or spend time on social media. Chris' miracle happening in February was a blessing, and I wanted to share this miracle as my Black History post. So, I logged into my profile and posted my one and only Black History fact.

I wrote, **"For the first time, I'm letting my friends state Black History facts. I can't do it this time! My only fact for Black History will be this: MY SON, Christopher Wright, WALKED TODAY FOR THE 1ST TIME!!!! I'm a happy mother!!! Those who know what happened to my son, this is a MAJOR accomplishment! That's my Black History Fact TODAY!!!!**

#GodDidThis #GodWithHim #Happy #PrayerWorks #Mom

Chapter 8

Turning Tides

About two weeks after the shooting, police detectives from the Columbia Police Department arrived to question Chris. They delayed the interview until Chris was off the ventilator and could talk. However, the hospital kept them abreast of his status, and they looked forward to finally speaking with him.

As they walked into his room, the detectives identified themselves and explained why they were there. They had already visited the apartment Chris shared with Darius and Kevin and questioned both roommates. The detectives also explored the neighborhood where the shooting occurred before arriving at the hospital. They took the time to knock on the neighbors' doors, but no one knew or saw anything that night. People admitted they heard the shots but didn't bother to look outside.

The detectives brought a search warrant for Chris' cell phone, hoping it would help them find the shooter. Like many other young black men, Chris disliked the police due to negative experiences. However, since I was in the room with him, Chris showed them respect and answered their questions. One detective asked Chris a series of personal questions.

He asked, "Do you smoke weed?"

Chris replied, "No."

Then he asked, "Do you sell weed or drugs?"

Chris again replied, "No."

The detective asked, "Do you have a girlfriend?"

Chris said, "No."

Finally, the detective asked, "Do you have a beef with anyone?"

Chris answered firmly, "NO."

Everything added up to the fact that Chris led a quiet life that consisted of work and home, which proved to the detectives that no one had a reason to target him.

I didn't take offense to Chris being treated with such suspicion. I raised my children well, but I'm also not dumb. Kids may sometimes do things their parents don't know about. Chris wasn't perfect, but thankfully, he had nothing to hide from me or the police.

The detectives told us they believed Chris was an innocent victim of a gang initiation. They found no evidence to suggest any other reason for the attack. The detectives assured us they didn't affiliate Chris with any gangs, drugs, or illegal activity. Sadly, Chris walking home that night in his work uniform possibly resembled gang colors. No one knew the mindset of the person or persons who shot my son. They could've watched Chris for months as he walked from the bus stop. There were so many scenarios, but the result was still the same. Someone shot Chris and left him for dead on the streets of Columbia.

Multiple gangs continue to be rampant in Columbia, South Carolina. Even now, as I write, gang-related shootings and killings continue to happen in Columbia and other cities throughout the United States, especially in African-American communities. Mothers like myself have grown weary and tired of the senseless shootings and killing of our loved ones.

Before they left the room, the detectives shared a few more details with us.

They said, "Unfortunately, we haven't found the gun used in the shooting or the shooter. You can pick up Chris' cell phone at the police station. We've both been assigned to this case, so call us with any questions."

They gave me their business cards and left. The possibility of Chris' case being a gang initiation made me doubt they would solve it. I thought about the detectives questioning people in the neighborhood, and the replies didn't surprise me. People are sometimes afraid to talk to the police about shootings. Maybe someone who saw something will call the CRIME STOPPERS number and give their information anonymously. Who knows? I was concerned it would take months or maybe years to find out who shot my son, or even worse, Chris' shooting would become a cold case with no arrest ever made.

Chris asked if I could stop by the police department to pick up his cell phone. So, the next morning, after leaving the hotel, I drove straight to the police station in Columbia. I used Google Maps for directions. As I drove, I saw Wood, King, and Tree streets. However, Tree Street stood out to me. I was tempted to turn onto the street but chose not to because I just needed to focus on retrieving my son's cell phone. I was concerned turning onto that street would awaken trauma and every emotion I wasn't ready to feel. I couldn't address my emotions and deal with Chris' hospital stay at the same time.

I had difficulty finding the entrance when I arrived at the police station. Once I found the door, I walked in and greeted the receptionist behind the plexiglass.

I said, "Good morning. I'm here to pick up my son's cell phone. His name is Christopher Wright."

She replied, "OK. In order to collect your son's belongings, I'll need to see your identification."

I handed her my driver's license, and she stepped away

from the desk. The receptionist returned shortly with a light brown envelope. She handed it to me, along with my license, through the glass. I could feel his cell phone inside the package, so I thanked her and swiftly walked out of the police station toward my car.

Once I was safely inside the car, I noticed the written details on the envelope. Chris' name and address were listed as the victim. The date and time I picked up the envelope and its contents were also handwritten on the outside. Since the assailant who shot my son was still at large, the offender was marked as unknown. But the two words "Attempted Murder" jumped off the envelope and pierced my heart!

I placed the envelope on the passenger seat of my car, closed my eyes, and paused to take a deep breath. Just to think about the crime of attempted murder gave me chills. But seeing the words written in black ink on an envelope containing my son's personal property made it too real. The attempted murder confirmed how serious Chris' situation was. It made me angry knowing there was a person out there who thought they got away with murder or attempted murder. My level of anger scared me. I was infuriated that the person was still out there, and I demanded justice for my son.

I gathered my emotions, pulled out of the lot, and proceeded to drive to the hospital. I knew my son was ready to see his phone again. Once I parked my car, I removed the cell phone from the envelope. I didn't want Chris to see the disturbing information that was written about him. I only needed him to focus on his healing.

In addition to a visit from the detectives, Chris' case manager with the State Office of Victim Assistance also stopped by. She sat with us in his room and helped me complete the application. She informed me the state of South Carolina had a victim compensation fund to help people like my son, who were victims of a crime. They assisted with hospital bills, lost compensation, medical or dental care, and funeral expenses. I didn't know how much Chris' hospital bill was going to be, but I knew it had the potential to be astronomical.

I welcomed all help and assistance for Chris that we could get. We finished the application, and the case manager prepared to leave.

She said, "You will receive letters from the agency about his application status. You can call me with any questions or concerns that come up. I've made a note of Chris' recovery time in my file, and I wish you both the best."

I replied, "Thank you for all your help."

As I watched the case manager leave the room, I felt I had accomplished something for Chris despite none of this being his fault. The application was another positive direction toward his healing. It was also less of a worry for me as the days turned into weeks. I pushed my concerns about the mounting hospital bills to the back of my mind in order to focus on Chris' recovery and didn't think about them anymore.

Nurse Karen helped Chris walk daily using his walker. We liked Nurse Karen as she made it obvious her primary concern was her patients and their well-being. Chris told me he saw an obvious difference between the other nurses and Nurse Karen. He felt the others were only there for the money and could tell the difference as soon as one of those types of nurses walked into the room.

Chris only liked two nurses, Nurse Karen and Nurse Tabitha, and would only speak with them. Nurse Karen was sweet and made sure Chris was comfortable as his health progressed. She also ensured he walked a bit and sat in his recliner in the room. Nurse Karen called the recliner "Chris' sitting station," as it was his resting place after a walk, and he took naps there with a sheet or blanket over him. She knew he was always tired of lying in bed, and sitting up or walking helped circulate his blood.

One day, I was in Chris' room when Nurse Karen came in with a walker in her hands.

Nurse Karen asked, "Chris, are you ready to walk today?"

Chris replied, "Yes."

I watched her help Chris out of his bed and move his IV machine to the side. Nurse Karen held the wound vac machine in her hand while they both set out to walk around the nurses' station. I was excited to see this for myself since Avery had already seen Chris walk, and I was finally getting to see Chris walk with my own eyes. I had my cell phone in hand and recorded Chris walking with ease. The other nurses in the trauma unit noticed Chris and encouraged him as he continued to walk down the hallway. They had watched him progress over the weeks from a critical condition to a miracle recovery.

Chris finished one lap around the nurses' station.

Nurse Karen asked, "Do you want to walk another lap?"

Chris replied, "I think I can do it."

This time, Chris walked without his walker, and it was a proud moment for me to witness this accomplishment. I noticed during the second lap he struggled with his left leg. It was dragging a little, but that wasn't his injured leg. It concerned me to see his foot drag when he walked without his walker. I wondered whether the issue would be a temporary or permanent situation for Chris. I worried a bit, but then I set the emotion aside.

Nurse Karen and I noticed Chris' energy was depleted, so I told him to take it easy. However, Chris was out of breath by the time he reached the end of the nurses' station. My son walked with enthusiasm, and I was elated and thankful! In my mind, I was willing him to walk. I felt like I was Chris' cheerleader, leading him to victory. The more he walked, the more I cheered. He proved he could walk with and without his walker, which was a God-given accomplishment for such a short period and a blessing to see.

AVERY WAS SCHEDULED to return to San Diego on February 10th. Having my son with me for a couple of weeks was a blessing because he encouraged me to be strong for all my children. Avery returned to the naval base and was certain his brother would heal completely from his injuries. He was thankful he got to see some of his brother's progress, and I promised to keep him posted on Chris' health. I was now alone with Chris in Columbia, and I stuck to my daily routine of hospital, hotel, errands, preparation, and an uncertain future.

Not long after Avery left, I arrived at the hospital one day to find Chris had moved to a shared room with three other patients because another trauma patient needed his former room. The nurse told me that Chris could return to his room as soon as it was no longer needed by anyone else. I walked into the shared room and noticed two patients: a Caucasian man named Shawn and an African-American teenage boy. It appeared the teenager suffered from a gunshot wound. He continually called out for his mother, even though the nurses tried to keep him comfortable. He was making it difficult to record his vital signs or anything else needed for his care. He yelled at the nurses, saying they were hurting him, and asked for his cell phone to call his mother. When his mother answered the call, he pleaded for her to hurry and get to the hospital.

Chris' bed was across from his, and the teenager was aggravating him.

Chris whispered, "He's acting like a whiny little baby. I've had to deal with far more than this young kid."

I noticed Chris didn't look well and asked, "Do you feel OK?"

Chris replied, "I'm ok. I just feel tired."

The other patient, named Shawn, was hit by a car and thrown 30 feet. It was a miracle he survived. He had a broken collarbone and other injuries, which left him in pain most of the time, so he called out for the nurse to give him medication. Shawn also requested a TV to watch sports. He didn't want to go to sleep, but he still asked the nurses for medication, another pillow, and help to go to the bathroom.

Chris didn't bother the nurses because he just wanted to get better and go home, but these two patients were annoying him. Shawn was comical, and the teenager was whiny. However, Chris did his best to ignore them. Shawn constantly called the nurses for multiple reasons.

The nurses' intercom responses were the same, "Yes, Shawn!"

Shawn took a liking to Chris after he noticed all my son did was lie in bed and observe everything. Once Shawn discovered Chris was a sports fan, he became more determined to obtain a TV for their room. Their first conversation was a simple one.

Shawn asked Chris, "Are you alright?"

Chris replied, "Yeah."

As I sat next to Chris' bed, nurse Karen came into the room. She noticed Chris was quieter than usual.

Nurse Karen asked me, "Does Chris like fruit?"

I replied, "Yes."

She said, "I'll be right back. I'm going to the cafeteria. I want to get him something to lift his spirits."

Nurse Karen returned to the room with a small container of fruit. Chris was glad to see the fruit and ate it silently. Karen checked on Chris' vitals and noticed he wasn't feeling well. Chris looked more tired than usual. His eyes were weary.

Nurse Karen asked, "Chris, do you feel ok?"

He shook his head and said, "No."

Nurse Karen lifted Chris' gown and saw his colostomy bag

was full of blood. She acted quickly, and before I could react, two doctors came into the room and confirmed Chris was bleeding internally again. They reviewed his chart, noted the medication he was on, and scheduled a CT scan. Chris became mad when they told him he had to stop eating the fruit he was enjoying.

Nurse Karen felt sorry for him because Chris never complained while he waited for the scan. He kept saying he was tired and wanted to go home. Chris was tired of the hospital. He was tired of being sick. He was just plain tired and ready to give up.

I looked at him and said, "We came this far, and we are not giving up now. Please don't give up."

Chris kept repeating he was tired, and his words hurt me because only he knew what he was going through and how he felt. I watched his spirit wane, which was not a good sign. I feared he would let go. He had shown so much strength until that moment, never once complaining since he first arrived at the hospital. However, this time was different. He was exhausted and ready to give up on himself.

The nurse came into the room to wheel him away to surgery.

I reminded Chris, "I need you to be strong for me."

He nodded and said, "I will, momma."

After Chris was wheeled out of his room, I sat back down in the chair before I returned to the waiting area. I was unaware of how long it would be before Chris returned. I felt helpless again and desperately wanted to take away my son's pain. I fought back tears as I silently prayed to God to heal Chris from this setback.

Then I heard a voice say, "This too shall pass!"

No one was around me when I heard this.

I sighed and inwardly replied, "I hope it does. I really hope it does."

It was a heavy burden for me, as Chris' mother, to see him

endure so much. All he wanted was to heal and leave the hospital. He didn't ask to be there to begin with. To be honest, I was tired of being there myself, as it had unfortunately become a second home to me. I wanted to cry. I wanted to scream! All of this was so unfair, but not once did I question God. Not once did I ask God why He forsook us. Instead, I walked to the waiting area and once again waited for a report from Chris' doctors.

Chapter 9

Yay, We're Almost Home!!!

After the procedure to stop Chris' internal bleeding, it took a while for him to eat again. They placed him on a liquid diet for the first couple of days. Chris drank every option on the liquid menu, from soups to ginger ale and whatever else they allowed. He liked a specific brand of ginger ale, Seagram's, and drank it more than water. He said there was a taste difference between Seagram's and other ginger ale brands. So, it became his only request when the nurses took his drink order. Once permitted to have food, the first thing Chris requested was the fruit nurse Karen had brought to him before the surgery, along with everything else the doctors permitted. It didn't matter what it was; Chris just wanted food!

The frequency of visitors to the hospital lessened over the weeks as everyone returned to their daily lives. Chris showed tremendous progress in recovering from his injuries and surgeries. I still called my mother and sister with updates so they could forward the news to our family members and friends. During one of my update calls with my mother, she had news for me.

She said, "Your former boss, Mr. Vernon, stopped by to

find out how Chris was doing and left an envelope for you. I didn't open it, but I'll have Dawn bring it with her to the hospital this weekend."

I replied, "Thanks, Ma. I appreciate it."

When Dawn arrived at the hospital, she gave me the envelope from Mr. Vernon and several cards sent to me and Chris. To my surprise, there was money in all of them. People had heard what happened and sent monetary donations to assist with whatever we needed. My colleagues on the Georgetown campus gave us monetary donations as well. It was a tremendous help. Otherwise, I wouldn't have been able to stay in Columbia with Chris while he recovered. I carefully budgeted the money received for my stay and daily essentials.

Dawn's visit was full of humility and laughter as she kept Chris and I company. She, too, witnessed the shenanigans of Chris' hospital roommate Shawn. I called it shenanigans, but it really wasn't. He was hilarious, but I couldn't tell if he was serious or just making fun of his situation. Shawn called the nurses constantly, and each time, it was for something different. He said it was to keep them on their toes, but I think he got a kick out of their repeated response.

Every time he buzzed, the nurses replied with a hint of frustration, "Yes, Shawn!"

Shawn became my sister's entertainment. She chuckled each time the nurses came into the room to see what he wanted. They remained professional as they answered his questions and catered to his needs. After the nurses left the room, Shawn would turn to me and Dawn and strike up a conversation like nothing had happened. Even Chris joined in on the conversation.

Shawn was a cool dude despite his pain from being hit by a car and thrown 30 feet. Shawn nicknamed Chris "Buddy." I met Shawn's parents while sitting in the waiting room during one of Chris' many surgeries. At the time, Shawn was also undergoing surgery. We had a pleasant conversation while waiting for updates on our children's conditions.

Shawn's parents were nice people. After talking to Shawn's mother, I could tell where Shawn got his charisma and mannerisms. I only saw his parents twice in the waiting area, but our conversations were never boring. Shawn's mother was a retired nurse and seemed to have the inside scoop of the hospital. She once told me that multiple patients in the trauma unit were innocent victims of gun violence, just like Chris.

Dawn enjoyed her visit with us, thanks to Shawn. Shortly after Dawn left, nurse Tabitha walked into the room.

She said, "I need to check Chris' vitals and change his dressing."

The nurses constantly changed Chris' bandages and colostomy bag. Usually, I was not in the room. However, this time, I was, and I paid close attention to how she replaced the gauze on his abdomen. I knew this process would be my responsibility after Chris was discharged. I was unsure to what extent or how long I would be responsible for changing his dressings. Either way, I needed to learn. It would be my first time seeing Chris' stomach since his arrival at the hospital. So, I did my best to prepare for what I would see.

Nurse Tabitha retrieved all the necessary supplies before she began. She laid gauze pads, saline solution, wound vac sponges, scissors, and clear tape on the tray beside Chris' bed. Then she sanitized her hands and put on gloves before opening Chris' hospital gown, exposing a long incision covered with clear tape attached to the wound vac machine.

That day, I learned there are three methods of wound vac care and how they work. The wound vac machine helps heal the wound by applying a vacuum through a specially sealed dressing (the clear tape). The machine's purpose is to draw the fluid out of the wound and increase blood flow to the area. It's often used to treat and help heal wounds after laparoscopic surgery. In Chris' case, the wound vac would help heal his incision and close it, eventually leaving a thin scar. Cotton gauze best describes the method I saw used to close the incision. I asked nurse Tabitha about the process as I watched.

She explained, "The wound vac machine will help close Chris' skin without using staples."

I thought since his stomach was open to the extent it was, staples would've been rather painful and not as effective. When Chris first arrived at the hospital, I refused to view the mesh opening of his exposed intestines. I couldn't have that image etched in my brain for the rest of my life. I would have fainted if I saw five holes in his intestines. However, a small part of me wished I had looked at it just to have a comparison of how well he was healing.

Nurse Tabitha was the only nurse who showed me the opening, and I did my best to hide from Chris how mortified I was by the sight. The incision on his abdomen was midpoint from his chest to above his pubic hair, and it was at least an inch or two in width. It was difficult to find the words to explain what I saw. His incision resembled a bloody steak, except it wasn't a steak. It was his abdomen.

All I could think was, "How did my child survive all this?"

Chris looked directly in my face as the nurse worked. I knew he was using my expressions to judge how bad or good things really were. So, I did my best to act as normal as possible. I looked back at him, smiled, and gave him a thumbs-up to let him know I wasn't fazed. However, deep down, I was definitely affected. It looked painful, bloody, and gory, like a victim in a horror movie.

I watched Nurse Tabitha use different gauze to fit the opening. She placed saline solution on them and bundled them together to cover the incision. Then, the nurse cut the vac sponge to fit perfectly over the gauze. This part of the process was vital as it ensured Chris' incision would close. She positioned the cut vac sponges over the gauze, affixed the clear tape over it, and connected the sponge to the machine. After

Nurse Tabitha completed the process, I watched as blood slowly seeped through the tube into the vac machine, slowly working to close the skin.

Once finished, Nurse Tabitha collected the old dressings and threw them in the trash. She also checked Chris' colostomy bag, which was empty at the time. Then, she confirmed his IV line was fine. When all was done, she removed her gloves and sanitized her hands.

Nurse Tabitha asked, "Do either of you need anything?"

Chris and I both replied, "We're fine."

She said, "OK, I'll be back later to check on Chris."

Then, she walked out of the room.

I liked Nurse Tabitha because she took the time to explain everything to me. At some point, she realized I would likely become Chris' caregiver once the hospital discharged him. Chris also liked her because she showed patience and treated him with respect. Nurse Tabitha even let me help change out Chris' old dressing and cut the vac sponge.

One day, as I stood by Chris' bed watching her begin the process, she invited me to help.

Nurse Tabitha asked, "Do you want to help me?"

I said, "Sure, what do you want me to do?"

Nurse Tabitha guided me in changing the gauze with kind and sincere words. I was apprehensive at first, but Chris watched and encouraged me as I tried to understand how to help care for him.

After learning how to change the gauzes, I didn't talk to Chris about the experience. I sat next to his bed and tried to act like what I saw hadn't affected me. However, every time I closed my eyes, the etched memory of my son's raw incision was still there. The vision of his incision reminded me of the seriousness of each surgery and how close to death Chris had been. I knew it was the will of God that Chris survived. There is no other explanation for it.

THE FIRST WEEK of February arrived, and that Sunday, February 5th, was Super Bowl LI. Chris' favorite football team, the Atlanta Falcons, was scheduled to play the New England Patriots. Chris was ecstatic that his team was in the Super Bowl. Chris' first cousin, Shantine, also known as "Shan," stopped by just days before the game and brought gifts for Chris. One of them was a Falcons knit hat with a Pom, which became his favorite. He even placed the hat on his head before Shan left the room.

On the day of the Super Bowl, Shawn, Chris' hospital roommate, wanted to rest and gave Chris control of the TV to watch the game.

Shawn said, "Here's the TV remote. Enjoy the game. I'm going to sleep. I'll bug the nurses later."

That worked out because Chris' friend, Rico, stopped by to watch the Super Bowl with Chris. Since I didn't watch sports, I let him have that moment for himself and his friend. I took that time to take a break and relax at the hotel, a first since arriving in Columbia. Chris had a good time watching the Super Bowl with Rico, even though his team lost by six points.

After Super Bowl weekend, we received good news from the doctors. Chris was being moved to a regular room. No more trauma unit! Chris would move to a lower floor, which meant he was almost ready to go home. Knowing that the room change meant we were closer to the threshold of being discharged made me happy and relieved.

The week of February 13th, Chris officially moved into a regular hospital room. It was such a good feeling to know Chris had made significant progress. I thought he would be in the hospital longer, but God had other plans. Now, my thoughts shifted to whether or not I was ready to take care of him by myself once he came home. Self-doubt is a bad thing. Instead of encouraging myself, I talked myself out of things and reasoned why I couldn't do things. At times, I could be my worst enemy, and this was one of those times. I doubted my capabilities to care for my son, but I shouldn't have.

Raising and taking care of Chris and his siblings differed from what I would have to do as a caregiver. Of course, there isn't any known manual for good parenting, and I discovered there really wasn't a manual for being a good caregiver either. I watched my mother take care of my stepfather for years, and like myself, she hit the ground running in patient care. By "hit the ground running," I mean she jumped in to care for his every need without being formally trained. My stepfather had suffered several strokes, and the last couple of strokes left him bedridden. His care needs went from moderate to extreme.

Chris' needs were different, and I believed he would only need moderate care for a short period. However, there was no real way to determine his needs until he was discharged from the hospital. Then, his needs would be assessed based on where he was in the recovery process in terms of wound care and rehabilitation. As his mother, his needs and recovery had to trump my fear of whether I'd be a good caregiver or not.

As we prepared to move to the new room, the nurse said, "Be sure to bring all of his belongings to the new room."

I nodded in agreement and replied, "Ok, but he doesn't have much since he's been in hospital gowns and socks for a month."

Chris asked, "Mama, where are my clothes?"

I said, "You don't have any clothes here."

He insisted, "Yes, I do. My street clothes should be in the room."

I got frustrated and asked the nurse, "Do you know where the clothes are that he wore to the hospital?"

The nurse said, "The previous hospital cut them off the night of the shooting to access his wounds."

Chris said, "Mama, I had just bought my white sneakers."

I sternly looked at him and replied, "You can replace your sneakers and clothes, but not your life."

I used a firm tone to imply that he needed to drop the subject because the clothes didn't matter. Those clothes held no value over his invaluable life.

A short time later, another nurse came to take Chris to his new room. Right away, I could see in Chris' demeanor that he didn't like her. I quickly flashed him that motherly look that nonverbally told him to stop being like that. She was just doing her job, at least that's what I wanted to believe, even though she appeared a little skittish. I wasn't sure if she was new or still being trained. However, I'm sure Chris made her nervous. The facial expressions he gave her would make anyone anxious.

The nurse helped him into the wheelchair, and we all left the room we had come to know so well. As I walked behind them toward the elevator, the nurse opened the hall door and hit Chris' right leg! The same knee and leg he had been shot in and was still healing. Chris looked like he wanted to hit her. I know she messed up badly, but she immediately apologized to him.

While we waited for the elevator, the nurse tried to have a conversation with Chris, but he wasn't having it.

He looked at her like, "Stop talking to me."

He dismissed her entire existence because she hurt his leg. He really wanted her to leave him alone.

I looked at her and replied, "He's just tired and ready to take a nap."

Chris shot me a look that reflected his frustration with my response.

His look silently shouted, "You know why I'm not talking to her!"

Once we got off the elevator and wheeled Chris to his new room, I noticed how nice and quiet it was without the glaring lights and sounds of the trauma unit equipment. It seemed quaint.

The nurse got Chris settled in bed and ensured he was comfortable. He took full advantage of being able to sleep the way he wanted without tubes attached. Chris no longer had Nurse Karen or Tabitha, and it felt weird to be on a regular hospital floor without them. We didn't get the chance to say goodbye or thank Nurse Karen and Tabitha for taking good care of him. I knew it was their job, but they made Chris' time in the trauma unit run smoothly, even with the slight hiccup of internal bleeding along the way.

I sat down next to the bed while Chris slept. I stayed a good while before I returned to the hotel room for the night. It elated me to know it wouldn't be long before they discharged my son, and we were on our way home. This time, I wasn't worried about if he would have a rough night because he had progressed so well. Chris seemed almost normal except for the colostomy bag on his side.

I was exuberant because Chris was in a regular room, but my mind wasn't fully at peace yet. I thought about all that happened and all we had been through as a family. Don't get me wrong, the mother in me was thankful but also tired and weary from the toll it took on me.

Before sleep took over, I quickly prayed, "God, please bless Chris to have a good restful night and give me peace of mind."

The next day, when I arrived at the hospital, I fought the urge to go to the trauma unit. It had been my routine for weeks. Since I wasn't sure if I would see Nurse Karen or Tabitha, I went ahead and took the elevator to Chris' new floor. The nursing assistant, whom Chris didn't care for, approached me as soon as I stepped out of the elevator. She had a snippy attitude, which also caused me not to like her very much as well.

She said, "Chris just lies in the bed and won't interact with me when I walk in his room. I think he's depressed from being in the hospital. He won't do any physical activity like walking to help himself recover."

I looked at her as she continued with her assumptions about my son. Based on her comments, I assumed she was basing her opinions on what she had read in his chart. How could this young woman stereotype my son and assume he was in a gang, depressed, or had led a terrible life? The more she talked, the more her assumptions irritated me.

I waited until she finished speaking and said, "Thank you for your concern. I will talk with Chris about depression."

Then, I briefly explained to her what happened to Chris. I was certain he wasn't depressed and wanted to put the tech's assumptions to bed.

I walked into Chris' room, still irritated by this young woman's assumptions about him. We need to put an end to the harmful practice of cultural stereotyping! Not all young black men are in trouble.

I sat down in the recliner next to his bed and noticed Chris sleeping peacefully on his side with the covers over his head. To sleep on our sides is normal to us. However, it was a luxury for Chris since the tubes had prevented him from doing so for almost a month. I turned the TV on to entertain myself while he slept, and it wasn't long before he woke up. I thought about the conversation I had in the hall with the young woman and decided to ask the hard question.

I asked, "Chris, are you depressed?"

Chris replied, "No, mama. I'm not depressed at all."

I shared with him the conversation I had with the nursing assistant.

Chris said, "Mama, I just want to be left alone, especially by her. She has a bad attitude and gets on my nerves. All the other nursing assistants and nurses that come in here are fine. But she constantly walks in to check my vitals when I'm trying to rest. And she does it every time right when I finally get to sleep! I know it's her job. I'm just sleepy, not depressed."

I nodded my head to show I understood him. This particular nursing assistant walked in with an air about her that didn't mix with Chris. This made her unapproachable in Chris' eyes. That's why he preferred not to deal with her, and the best way to do that was not to acknowledge her unless he had to. Not to say it was right or wrong, but I totally understood where he was coming from. I didn't like the assumption she made, and I chose not to share her exact words with Chris. However, I was relieved to know he wasn't depressed.

So, I replied, "If you ever feel depressed, I'm here for you. You've gone through so much this last month, and that can be a lot to process and deal with. So, I'm here to listen, or I can arrange for a counselor anytime. I'm your mother and will always be here for you, so you can tell me if you ever need to talk."

Chris reassured me, "Mama, I'm fine," then turned to the other side and went back to sleep.

A couple of days later, the doctors told us they would discharge Chris from the hospital on February 20th. I was ecstatic and petrified at the same time. Now, I would be Chris' caregiver and responsible for his care. No nurses, just me! The next day, a medical supply representative stopped by the room to measure Chris for a brace for his left leg. Chris' left leg and ankle were weak, so the brace would support him.

The representative said, "You'll need to buy Chris a pair of thick socks and a pair of good sneakers. The brace will fit in his shoe and secure around his left leg to support him since he's currently walking with a limp."

I hadn't seen Chris walk much since he moved to the regular hospital floor. When he did, it was limited walks to the bathroom. I was concerned that he may have nerve damage in his leg. Although his left leg was not injured, his ankle wouldn't move. I watched Chris lift his left foot to walk the short distance to the bathroom and wondered if his limp would be permanent. Truthfully, I prayed he would recover even if it wasn't 100 percent. The doctors wouldn't confirm when the limp would go away.

They just said, "His body went through a lot of trauma. It's going to take time for his left leg and body to heal. There's no definitive time we can give you."

After the representative finished the assessment, I immediately left the hospital and drove to a local department store to purchase sneakers. If any adjustments needed to be made to Chris' brace, I wanted to ensure it could be done without delay.

I found the perfect black and red sneakers and sent a picture of them to Chris for his approval. With Chris' yes, I purchased them and some socks. Then, I drove back to the hospital in time for the representative to return with the brace. He helped Chris with his socks, secured the brace on Chris' left leg, and helped him put his foot in the sneakers. Everything fitted with no adjustments needed!

The representative asked Chris, "Do you want a walker because the hospital can send you home with one?"

I told Chris, "Get the walker."

Reluctantly, Chris agreed. Then, the representative left the room for a moment.

Chris said, "I'm not walking with a walker. I want a cane. The walker will make me look like an old man."

So, we compromised. Upon his discharge, we would leave with the walker, and I would buy him a cane from the CVS store on my way to the hotel. The cane would already be in the car for the ride home from the hospital.

Chris said, "I'm placing the walker in the corner as soon as we get home because I'm not using it. I just want the cane. It'll be better for me."

True to his word, he never used the walker, only the cane. I think he felt it made him look sickly, and he didn't want to receive pity from anyone.

The following day, Dorothy, a nurse who specialized in wound ostomy care, came to Chris' room. She was to show me the correct way to care for Chris' stoma and change the skin barrier and pouch. She placed the moldable stomahesive accordion flange skin barrier, pouch, alcohol wipes, protective adhesive barrier wipes, and a couple of washcloths on Chris' bed. Every procedure for his care began and ended with hand washing.

As she started the process, she explained, "You must be sure to clean his stoma properly and place a new barrier and pouch around it. Here is a booklet. I've already marked the pages of supplies needed for Chris' stoma care. You'll want to call the representative to reorder when you notice you're running low to ensure you don't go days without everything you need."

Nurse Dorothy made it sound really easy as she explained the process. Well, it didn't seem simple to me as a beginner learning something totally out of my field of expertise. Everything Nurse Dorothy said overwhelmed me.

I thought, "Why do I have to do this? Why can't a nurse come to the house?"

I got scared as my caregiver role became more real. We weren't told how long Chris would have the stoma and whether it would be temporary or permanent. If the nurses did tell us, I couldn't remember because I was too busy freaking out about my son's ostomy care. I looked at Nurse Dorothy and Chris calmly, but internally, I was having a meltdown. I didn't want to learn anything other than changing the gauze on his right leg and abdomen.

Nurse Dorothy went to the sink and placed lukewarm water in a small mauve-colored hospital pan after we discussed how to order supplies.

She said, "You must empty the colostomy bag before you remove it."

After removing the barrier and bag, the nurse placed them in a small garbage bag on the bedside table. She used an alcohol wipe to remove the adhesive barrier from his skin. Then Nurse Dorothy soaked the clean washcloth in water, wrung it, and cleaned around the stoma site. She retrieved a dry washcloth and proceeded to pat dry around the stoma area.

She explained, "You must clean the area around the stoma before applying the protective barrier."

The stomahesive accordion flange skin barrier was moldable and needed to be molded to ensure a proper fit around the stoma. Nurse Dorothy placed the barrier over the stoma and used her thumb to move it to different spots. She molded it perfectly and placed it in the correct form.

The nurse said, "We must correctly mold the barrier because once the stoma expels waste, the waste will fall into the pouch. If not done properly, there'll be a mess to clean, and you'll need to replace the barrier."

Nurse Dorothy placed the stoma flange skin barrier around the stoma, peeled the back off the skin barrier, and placed the barrier around the stoma perfectly. The end of the pouch was then closed and secured.

After Nurse Dorothy finished the steps, she said, "Okay, now it's your turn to show me if you were paying attention. If you get the steps right, Chris can go home."

Chris and I looked at each other, and Chris said, "Mama, you can do it!"

In my head, I replied, "Thanks, Nurse Dorothy, for putting me on the spot."

Nurse Dorothy said, "I am confident you can do it."

The look on my face showed my lack of confidence and uncertainty about this new routine. In my mind, it was imperative I performed each step correctly because Chris and I wanted to go home. Both of us were tired of being in the hospital, and financially, I didn't know how much longer I could stay in Columbia. We both had enough of Columbia and were ready to go home.

Since she had only shown me the process once, I wasn't sure if I would miss a step or pass. I took a deep breath, said a silent prayer, and correctly performed every step Nurse Dorothy showed me. I surprised myself, but then again, that was God! Chris watched me perform every step and didn't say a word. I believe he internally willed me to pass Nurse Dorothy's test.

I was so relieved when she said, "Mama, you did it! You passed, and Chris can go home!"

Then Chris said, "Good job, Mama!"

He gave me two thumbs up, and that's when I knew I could properly care for Chris by myself.

Nurse Dorothy shared a few hacks to care for the pouches when I needed to wait for the replacement pouches to arrive.

She said, "The pouches are reusable and cleanable. You can clean them with cold water and denture cleanser tablets. Soak it for a while, move the pouch around in the cold water, remove it from the hospital pan, and hang it to dry with a clothespin. It also helps to squirt one or two sprays of cooking oil (Pam) in all clean or new bags, so when bodily waste enters the bag, it will go straight in and easily slide out into the toilet after you cut the bag open. You can use baby wipes to clean the bag before closing."

The nurse and I cleaned our hands before she walked out of the room. Some years later, I met a gentleman who had a stoma, and I shared her helpful hacks with him.

After I passed my test with Nurse Dorothy, a nurse didn't return to Chris' room until after lunch. Chris ate his last lunch, sat fully dressed on the bed, and waited impatiently to leave. I sat in the chair next to Chris and quietly celebrated passing the test. I felt like I was on cloud nine. I believe God made it happen. He guided me in performing the ostomy care steps correctly. I was happy because I got the procedure right on the first try, which was important to me.

The nurse finally returned with Chris' discharge papers, prescriptions, walker, and supplies. She handed me 28 pages of information about his condition and instructions for his care. The directives included prescribed medications, wound care, stoma cleaning, and changing the colostomy pouch. It overwhelmed me as I started reading through each document. I skimmed through what I needed to look over but promised myself I would thoroughly go over every page once settled at home.

The nurse said, "You can take everything, including his walker, to the car and drive around to the front entrance. Chris and I will meet you out front."

She helped Chris sit in the hospital wheelchair and ensured he was comfortable. By the time I drove my car to the front entrance and got out, the nurse was already there with Chris. She helped Chris out of the wheelchair, and I handed him the cane I had kept in the car. He stood up and carefully walked to the passenger side.

Chris focused on every step he took. My son looked so fragile and sickly. It appeared he used all his energy to walk the few steps to my car. I refrained from telling Chris how frail he looked because he had been through enough. He didn't need to be reminded or told about his current condition. I secured Chris in the car while ensuring the seat belt didn't restrict his colostomy bag. I walked back to the driver's side and quickly got in as the nurse wished us well. I drove away, grateful to be leaving the hospital with my son. We made it, God! We made it!

Chapter 10

Please, Not Again!!!

As the view of the hospital became smaller and smaller in my rear-view mirror, the words on Chris' discharge papers consumed my emotions. They printed the reason for his hospital admission in bold letters.

It read, **"Acute blood loss anemia; Acute pain due to trauma; Assault with GSW (gunshot wound); Melena; Open abdominal wall wound; presence of colostomy; S/P exploratory; Traumatic hemorrhagic shock."**

The bold letters reiterated the seriousness of his injuries, just like our FMLA forms a month earlier. I'm still in awe of how he survived all that.

I briefly looked over Chris from head to toe while I drove. I noticed his hair was thinning on the top of his head, and he appeared skinnier than usual. I think seeing him in regular clothes made it more obvious to me. He looked haggardly and sickly, but again, he had been near death, and his skinny body had fought a good fight and won. But that was ok because Bri and I would fatten him up somehow.

Bri took over my kitchen after she enrolled in culinary classes at her high school. I was more than happy to let her take over. Now that Chris was coming home, she would be a big help while I took care of Chris. I knew she would rather cook than change his gauze. I knew I could stomach more than her. She hadn't seen his wounds or colostomy bag yet.

Chris called Darius while we drove and said, "Hey, I'm on my way to the apartment to pick up my things. I'm staying with my mom for a while. Are you there?"

Darius replied, "Yeah, we're here. Where are you?"

Chris said, "I just left the hospital, so we'll be there shortly."

Chris hung up and guided me to the apartment. I noticed their complex was in the same area as the police station. When we arrived, Darius and Kevin came outside to greet Chris, and I saw the look of concern on Darius' face. Darius saw what I saw. Chris appeared sickly and ultra-thin, and when he walked, he slouched and stepped as though he could barely walk. I caught Darius' glance and shook my head, silently asking him not to say anything about Chris' appearance. We both knew how gaunt he looked.

I said, "I'm going to sit in the car and wait while you guys grab Chris' things."

I knew they needed their time to catch up. I watched as Darius helped Chris walk with his cane toward the apartment. Darius stayed next to Chris to give him physical support as they walked in together. While I sat in the car and listened to music, I noticed the public library was across the street. I observed how quiet the neighborhood was and watched cars drive by while I waited for Chris and Darius.

It wasn't long before they walked out of the apartment building and slowly headed toward my car. Darius carried Chris' bag and observed him as he walked. I gave Darius a hug after he placed the bag in my car and tried to assure him.

I said, "Chris is making good progress and on the road to recovery. Thank you for being a good friend, and I appreciate you being there for him. He'll be fine and will fully recover."

I understood the look on Darius' face as he took in Chris' condition. We all needed to believe this was temporary. Chris was alive, walking, and ironically, not in any pain!

My GPS app led me to drive the back roads to Pawleys Island. Chris couldn't help me with directions because he fell asleep. He woke up periodically, only to see that I was still driving. At first, I thought we were lost and would need to turn back and start over. But, eventually, it led me to Highway 51 through Georgetown and into Pawleys Island. Finally, we were home!

I parked my car, retrieved Chris' cane from the back seat, and helped him out of the car. He stood up for a minute, reached for his cane, and slowly walked inside the house. Bri and Money both came to the door to greet Chris. Bri made a fruit tray for him that spelled out, Welcome Home. I thought it was the sweetest gesture. She and Money talked to Chris until he fell asleep on the couch with the fruit tray by his side. I watched him sleep and embraced how amazing it felt to have him home with us.

I had two bedrooms in my townhouse, and they were both located upstairs. Chris couldn't climb the stairs yet, so he slept in the living room on an airbed. We made sure it was comfortable for him, but I'm sure anything was better than a hospital bed. My living room looked like a hospital room minus the specialty bed. I organized his medications on the table based on their dosage time. Some needed to be given throughout the day and others at night. I didn't want to mess up giving him the wrong medicine. I needed to be certain every time.

I placed the gauze, saline solution, tape, washcloths, wipes, barriers, and pouches on a shelf below the table. This made it easy for me to grab them when I changed his dressings and colostomy bag. I arranged my little setup to make it easy for me to maneuver around the room. I was the only one changing his gauze and colostomy bags, as Money and Bri had left Chris' care to me. I truly believe everyone in the house preferred it that way.

The cost of colostomy supplies was not cheap, and I paid out-of-pocket until my insurance covered the expense. Chris' skin was sensitive, so I purchased Huggies Natural Care Sensitive Baby Wipes. They were fragrance-free to ensure they did not irritate his skin since he used them to clean around his stoma. We poured a small amount of mouthwash into the bag to remove the poop smell. This hack helped me for an entire year and a half until Chris had his colostomy reversal surgery. In an email, I thanked Nurse Dorothy for helping me care for Chris's stoma. She would've been very proud of my work. In true essence, I was proud of my work.

Chris' energy level reminded me of a baby. As his caregiver, I noticed he fell asleep at the drop of a hat. He slept after eating, taking medication, gauze changes, and emptying his colostomy bag. So, I took a nap whenever Chris napped. It all reminded me of when I first became a mother.

The first thing my mother told me as a new mom was, "When the baby takes a nap or goes to sleep, so do you."

Her advice still applied, even in this situation. When he woke up from his nap, I would hear the TV and walk downstairs to see if he needed anything. If Chris was hungry, I fixed him something to eat and checked his colostomy bag. Then, I left him alone to watch TV while I worked on my grad school assignments.

Bri had an early withdrawal her senior year and came home around lunchtime. Thankfully, she cooked for Chris whenever I overslept. Bri regularly cooked meals for her brother, and Chris looked forward to eating every dish she prepared. I was glad to let her cook because I was exhausted. I believe cooking was a welcomed distraction for Bri, so she didn't have to focus on Chris' wounds. I watched Bri's face change when she saw me change Chris' colostomy bag or his dressing. She struggled with what happened to her brother.

I gave Chris his medication for the night, changed his gauze, checked his colostomy bag, and asked if he needed anything before we all went to bed each night. If he didn't have any additional needs, I walked upstairs to my bedroom and took a shower. I would immediately fall asleep like I had just worked a 12-hour shift. We made it through the first night home, and the following became our routine for the week:

- Fix Chris' breakfast.
- Bri prep lunch and dinner for the next day.
- Give him morning medications.
- Change his gauze and colostomy bag.
- Take a nap.
- Fix his lunch.
- Work on my schoolwork.
- Give Chris a snack.
- Serve his dinner.
- Give him night medications.
- Check his colostomy bag and gauze.
- Go to bed for the night.

What I dealt with the first night didn't compare to our first week home, which was not for the fainthearted. Chris' abdomen still looked like a raw steak when I changed the gauze each day. But thankfully, his incision and wounds were slowly closing. I also noticed the scar tissue from the exit wound on his right thigh wasn't smooth. It appeared when the bullet exited his thigh, and it left a zigzag-shaped scar. I replaced the gauze on his right knee, where the doctors had removed an additional bullet. I became numb to the condition of Chris' right thigh and abdomen in order to focus on his healing.

On February 25th, I received the sweetest surprise. Chris walked upstairs into my room by himself! We had only been home a week, and Chris had been unable to walk up the stairs. But that day, he walked into my room with his cane and stood in my doorway.

I thought, "Oh my God! Did your sister help you up the stairs?"

Before I could ask, Chris said, "Mama, I walked up the stairs by myself. Well, with the help of my cane."

I was so happy and congratulated him for successfully walking up the stairs. Since I missed the miracle, I videoed Chris as he walked down the stairs with the help of the rail and his cane. He was a little out of breath afterward but proud of himself as he should've been. He accomplished a milestone within his first week of being home, and I was equally proud of him.

I said, "Chris, you still need to take it easy and try not to do too much at once. You've only been home a week, and your body is still recovering."

A couple of hours later, Chris called out for me.

He yelled, "Mama, come here! My bag is filling up with blood!"

Oh my God, not again! The same issue happened in the hospital. I called the nurse's service and informed them of Chris' blood-filled colostomy bag. The nurse told me to take him to the hospital immediately. Money, Bri, and I went into panic mode because we didn't know what was happening with Chris. Chris tried to dress himself, but he moved slowly and didn't look well. He looked exhausted. I helped put his shoes on his feet and checked his bag, and it was full of blood.

I removed the bag, placed a white washcloth over his

stoma, and grabbed a new colostomy bag to snap onto the barrier. Chris stood up with his cane and walked outside the car at a snail's pace. It looked like he wasn't moving at all or in slow motion until he finally reached the passenger side of my car. I looked him in the eyes and could tell he was about to faint.

I cried out to Money as he approached the car, "Money, catch Chris. He's about to faint!"

Money ran over and caught Chris before he fell to the ground. He placed him in the car, and I drove like a NASCAR driver to Waccamaw Hospital.

I asked myself, "Didn't I just see my son walk upstairs to my room? What happened? Did he overexert himself?"

It scared me all over again, thinking something was seriously wrong because his bleeding was a repeat of Palmetto Hospital. I exhausted my brain, replaying the scenario of Chris almost fainting by the car door. The whole situation petrified me out of my mind. I prayed I would make it to the hospital in time and that my son wouldn't die. I held back my tears and sped up because I didn't want my son to die on the way.

I prayed, "Please, God, don't let him die on the way to the hospital. Please, let me get Chris to the hospital without being stopped by the police!"

It was urgent for us to get Chris to the hospital, so I drove with the hazard lights on, but I refused to reduce my speed.

While we traveled, Chris' colostomy bag overflowed and spilled a bit in the passenger seat. I parked in front of the emergency room entrance of Waccamaw Hospital, and Money ran inside to grab a wheelchair. He opened the passenger door, scooped my son in his arms, and placed him in the wheelchair. The colostomy bag fell off Chris, and blood drenched the passenger seat.

Chris said, "Mama, the bag!"

I replied, "Chris, it's ok. Don't worry about that."

Money raced to get him inside because he was still bleeding out. I could smell blood as it poured straight down into the carpet underneath the passenger seat. This setback to his recovery made me feel helpless. I locked the car, ran inside the hospital, and Money met me at the door.

He said, "Chris is in the back. You go be with him, and I'll get the car cleaned."

I gave the receptionist the information she needed and rushed down the hallway to be with Chris.

My son looked so sickly like he did when he had internal bleeding at Palmetto Richland. Chris was hooked to an IV and given a new colostomy bag while we waited for the doctor. The bleeding had slowed a bit. Chris fell asleep, and I sat and watched him while we waited for the doctor.

When the doctor finally walked into the room, he said, "I'm sorry, but we're not equipped to treat gunshot wound victims. We've arranged for Chris to be transported to Grand Strand Medical Center in Myrtle Beach."

The doctor's news disappointed me, but I was thankful the ambulance arrived shortly after his visit. The paramedics secured Chris in the ambulance and sped off towards 82nd Avenue. It was my first time riding in an ambulance, but the paramedics made us feel at ease. Chris didn't recall his first ambulance ride after the shooting because they sedated him during his transport from Baptist to Richland.

The older paramedic was nice and talked to Chris about sports while I sat in the front with the younger paramedic.

He asked, "Have you ever ridden in an ambulance before?"

I replied, "No, not before today."

The look on my face revealed my anxiety, so the paramedic kept me calm by talking to me the entire way. I felt comfortable enough to share what happened to Chris, which justified the need to transport him to Grand Strand. I talked and laughed with the paramedic until we finally arrived at

Grand Strand Medical Center. The younger paramedic wished us luck before we got out of the ambulance, and I thanked him for being so nice to me.

I followed Chris and the paramedics through the emergency entrance. They informed the hospital staff of our arrival and Chris' condition. An ICU room was prepared for Chris shortly after, and it resembled his previous hospital room at Palmetto Health. I walked in and saw only a bench chair for visitors but no recliner for sleeping. That was my cue that I wouldn't be able to sleep in his room. I could only stay long enough for visiting hours and return the following day. I would also need to leave his room during nurse shift changes.

Each hospital was different, so I followed whatever rule applied. The only difference between being at Grand Strand and Palmetto Richland was my drive time. I only lived twenty-five minutes from Grand Strand and two hours from Richland. I didn't want to leave Chris, but the attending nurse assured me he was in excellent hands. She took my cell phone number to notify me in case anything happened. Before leaving the hospital, I called Shawn, Chris' father, to let him know what was going on with our son. I couldn't hide the overwhelming fear in my heart.

I said, "They're performing tests right now to try and identify the source of his internal bleeding. This really feels like déjà vu, doesn't it?"

Shawn replied, "Yeah, it does. I'm gonna get there as soon as I can, but please try to calm down. I can hear the worry in your voice."

I hung up with Shawn and walked over to Chris' bed.

I said, "I'm leaving now, but I'll be back early in the morning. I love you, and I know you're in excellent hands."

I kissed Chris' forehead. He nodded his head in response and fell asleep. Then, God and I had a personal conversation on my drive home.

I prayed, "God, I need Your guidance and strength, and I

rebuke this setback in Jesus' name. You've brought Chris so far, and I don't want to dwell on the problems. Lord, I need Your help."

I didn't feel the need to cry, but I felt a little defeated because Chris had only been home for five days. I doubted my care of him and blamed myself that he was back in the hospital, even though I knew it wasn't my fault. I knew I had done everything right, and Chris was in caring hands with not just me but Money and Bri. I then realized the devil was in my thoughts, and I rebuked the negative ideas and insecurities in Jesus' name. My son would have told me if I wasn't doing something right. I made myself laugh at the thought of that. Still, deep down, I needed them to stop his internal bleeding permanently in order for him to fully recover.

I updated Money and Bri on Chris' condition when I arrived home. I planned to drive back to the hospital in the morning to sit with him. The déjà vu feeling continued because I had to call my mother and sister to inform them that Chris was back in the hospital. I entrusted my mother and sister to inform our family because I was too tired to do it myself and needed to go to bed. Lastly, I texted Avery to let him know about Chris. I told him not to worry because I left his brother in capable hands.

After I set aside all I would need for the next day, I finally laid down for the night. My mind ran through the events of our day. As I slowly faded to sleep, I said a prayer.

I prayed, "God, please bless Chris to sleep well and not experience any more complications. Keep my son safe, and give him permanent healing. In the name of Jesus, Amen."

I woke up the next day with Chris on my mind as I prepared for the drive to Grand Strand. I waited until Bri and Money left for school and work, then got on the road. I was thankful for the shorter drive and looked forward to seeing my son. When I arrived, Chris' nurse gave me an update that was music to my ears.

She said, "Chris had a great night. One of his medicines and aspirin were the culprits for the GI bleed, and tests confirmed he didn't have blood clots. The doctor has taken him completely off both medications. He's been prescribed a different daily treatment, and we've already scheduled a follow-up appointment with his primary care doctor for March 7th."

While the nurse was checking his vital signs and colostomy bag, I noticed Chris had a bump on the left side of his stomach near his pelvic area.

I asked her, "I've never noticed this bump before. What is it?"

She replied, "They're bullet fragments."

She noted the confused look on my face and further explained.

She continued, "The bullet fragments aren't a threat to Chris. The doctors at Palmetto Health felt they didn't need to be removed. It could actually cause additional health issues and damage if we tried to remove them. It could take a year or more, but at some point, they will expel themselves. He'll be fine and discharged in a couple of days. He's already shown improvement on the new medication we gave him to control and eliminate the GI bleed."

I was thankful to hear the good news. Thank you, God!

After our conversation, I wondered how I overlooked the bullet fragments. I changed Chris' gauzes every day for a week and never noticed them. Then I realized Chris had been wearing boxers since he was home, which covered the bump. It horrified me to find out there were bullet fragments in his body. It was another unfortunate reminder of what he had been through.

My son didn't need to go through anything else. He had dealt with so much trauma in over a month, and not once did he complain, cry, or feel sorry for himself. Chris took it all in stride and looked at me for guidance and care. I think that's why I took every setback personally. It seemed like every step forward had so many steps back that led to the unknown. At least this time, it was fixable and required only a few days in the hospital. Chris already looked so much better than before.

As I sat with him, we fell back into our usual routine. Chris watched TV while I texted our family and friends. This time, I brought my Kindle to read books until he fell asleep. I took over the TV remote and watched comedy shows while he napped.

I relayed the good news of Chris' discharge to my family and friends. I also texted my best friend, Elanda, who lived 10 minutes from the hospital.

She replied," I'll stop by to check on you guys."

On Sunday afternoon, Elanda walked into Chris' room as I sat on the bench. Her presence was a welcomed distraction from my thoughts. I explained Chris' condition to her and that the bullet fragments were still in his body. Elanda took one look at me and knew I wouldn't leave Chris unless she pushed me.

She asked, "Have you eaten lunch yet?"

I replied, "No."

Elanda said, "Let's go, we're going to get something to eat. Besides, you need fresh air."

Elanda wouldn't take no for an answer.

She repeated herself as she walked toward the door, "Come on, let's go!"

Chris agreed with Elanda and said, "Mama, I'll be fine. Go get something to eat."

I reluctantly got up and put on my jacket to leave. We took the elevator to the first floor and walked toward the exit. As we walked through the lobby, I noticed a familiar face.

I looked at Elanda and said, "That looks like Dr. Fore, the president of Horry Georgetown Technical College (HGTC), my employer."

Elanda had a puzzled look on her face. We observed Dr.

Fore and her husband, who was also a doctor, in conversation with another couple. I slowly approached Dr. Fore.

I said, "Hi, Dr. Fore!"

She turned in my direction and said, "Hi, Shawn!"

I explained why I was at the hospital, and she introduced me to her husband and reminded him about Chris. Her husband held my hand the entire time we spoke as I stood between them.

Before we walked away, he said, "We're praying for Chris' recovery and for God to bless you both."

I thanked them both, and then Elanda and I walked out of the building. It was such a sweet interaction because it was my first time seeing President Fore outside of and meeting her husband. President Fore had seen me over the years but never outside the college, so the exchange warmed my heart. I wasn't aware she knew what happened to Chris. Honestly, I had no idea who all knew about our family's situation because I was still on FMLA leave.

Elanda and I had a wonderful lunch, and she did what she always does—she made me laugh! It didn't matter what we talked about; I could count on her to make me laugh. She drove me back to the hospital after our lunch.

She said, "I'm right down the street if you need me. Promise me you'll take care of yourself because I don't want you to get sick."

I replied, "I'm fine! I take my medication every day and eat when I can. Thanks for lunch."

We hugged goodbye, and I walked into the hospital feeling much better than earlier. The last thing I wanted was Elanda fussing at me about my health. My friends and family worried about me because they feared I wasn't taking care of myself. I wouldn't be able to help Chris if I got sick and needed care. It felt like everyone asked about my health and Chris' well-being. I appreciated their concern, but my focus was on Chris' discharge in the coming days.

Shawn, Chris' father, arrived the next day, and we resumed our hospital routine. He sat with Chris while I ran errands and ate lunch in the cafeteria. Shawn asked the nurses a lot of questions, just like he had done at Palmetto Health. I understood how he felt. He wanted to ensure Chris' healing would be permanent this time. Shawn stayed an additional few hours before his return to Atlanta.

The next day, February 28th, Chris was discharged from the hospital and looked much better. The nurses gave us new prescriptions and multiple pages of information. I promised to read them thoroughly once I was home.

I gave thanks to God as we drove away from the hospital. I was happy again! My son could continue to recover at home, and I could return to my routine as his caregiver—our new normal.

Chapter 11

Milestones

Once Chris and I had returned home, I noticed I needed to wake him up in the mornings to take his medicine.

He said, "I'm not sleeping at night. The nerves in my body keep moving around whenever I lay down."

I understood what he told me, but I thought maybe it was the nerves in his left leg that made him uncomfortable. The more he tried to explain the movement, the more I thought he was just strained from tossing and turning at night.

Chris exclaimed, "I'm going to call you later so you can see for yourself! This is driving me crazy, and I can't deal with this forever."

Lack of sleep and this weird issue made him irritable. Chris was concerned he would remain in a foul mood if the nerve problem continued to prevent his sleep.

Later that night, Chris called me downstairs. I stood by his bed; he threw the covers back, and I was shocked by what I saw – his nerves moved around in his left leg like a pinball machine. I couldn't believe what I had witnessed!

I thought, "No wonder the boy couldn't sleep. I wouldn't

be able to sleep either if my nerves moved up, down, and around my leg. I thought he was exaggerating when he said the muscles in his left leg moved around all night."

When I saw it for myself, I honestly thought it would expel his skin the way the nerves moved around. It was that bad.

I looked at Chris and said, "Oh my God! No wonder you can't sleep!"

He said, "See Mama! I can't sleep! The doctor has to prescribe something because I can't keep going through this!"

I replied, "Well, you have an appointment with Dr. Crosby in a couple of days, and we will see what he recommends. Hopefully, he can help you with this because you can't sleep like that."

Chris really needed to rest so his body could continue to heal and recover. I watched the nerves move in his leg until they finally settled down so Chris could fall asleep. He slept for a good bit until it started again and woke him up. I felt so sorry for him because all he wanted was to sleep and rest.

Luckily, on March 6th, Chris had a checkup with Dr. Crosby, our family's primary care physician, who has worked with us for over 20 years. He also had an appointment with Dr. Watson at Palmetto Health on March 9th. Whenever Chris needed to go to Palmetto Health, I took a day off from work to drive him to and from his appointment. It was the only time Chris went out in public. We usually stopped at a restaurant to order takeout after his appointments to avoid eating in public.

Chris still used a colostomy bag, which gave him no control over his bowels. He hated the smell of the waste and thought everyone else would hear or smell his bowels. But in actuality, he was the only one who knew or smelled anything. I believed he was subconscious about it and still felt uncomfortable. He dealt with the bag and smell when he was at home, but it was different in public.

Chris was ready for his appointment with Dr. Crosby. He put on his leg brace and grabbed his cane but looked exhausted from lack of sleep.

I reminded Chris, "Don't forget to inform Dr. Crosby about the muscle spasms you're experiencing throughout the night."

We drove to Waccamaw Medical Center (the building name at the time) in Georgetown and waited to see Dr. Crosby. Chris walked slowly after his name was called, and I sat with him in the examination room. Chris fell asleep in the chair while we waited, and I snuck a picture of him because he looked so peaceful. On cue, Dr. Crosby walked in with Chris' medical reports from Palmetto Health and Grand Strand Medical Center. He asked Chris to sit on the patient table so he could examine him.

Chris said, "I've been having muscle spasms in my leg at night that keep me from sleeping."

Dr. Crosby replied, "I'm going to suggest an over-the-counter medication which should lessen the spasms and allow you the much-needed sleep you lack. You are recovering very well, and your mom is taking great care of you."

It was their next conversation that touched my heart and almost brought tears to my eyes because it was very personal, genuine, and sincere.

Dr. Crosby smiled at Chris and asked, "Do you have questions?"

Chris replied, "No."

Dr. Crosby said, "I'm so glad you're still here with us."

Chris said, "So am I."

Then Dr. Crosby shook Chris' hand as we got up to leave the room.

We walked slowly to my car and discussed what Chris wanted to eat. I bought his food, stopped to purchase the recommended medication, and headed home. Chris ate his food once we got home. I made sure he was comfortable in his bed and gave him the medicine. He fell asleep like a toddler after I emptied his colostomy bag. I was thankful as he slept for a long time.

Chris' appointment with Dr. Watson at Palmetto Health was a few days later, and Bri came along with us. He still got tired from long-distance walks, so Bri found a wheelchair once we arrived. I signed in for Chris, and Bri didn't leave her brother's side. I secretly took a picture of them together in the waiting area. It was proof of how dedicated Bri was to her brother's needs.

Once we were called to be seen, Bri wheeled her brother into the room while I carried his cane. Dr. Watson came into the examination room and looked at Chris' incision.

The doctor said, "Chris, your wound is closing nicely into a thin line. Your stoma looks great, and overall, you're progressing well. Let's schedule an appointment to see you again in a couple of months."

I realized Chris' recovery period slowly progressed with each doctor appointment. I didn't rush it, and I was thankful for the positive feedback from both doctors. My caregiving skills improved as I learned to interpret Chris' needs without him uttering a word when he was in my presence. I didn't hover because it annoyed him when I treated him like he couldn't do for himself. I don't believe anyone in this situation would want to be treated like an invalid.

Chris said, "Mama, I feel bad that I need to lie in bed most of the time."

I reminded him, "Your body must recover from the intense trauma you endured. Your body needs to rest and take time to heal. So it's okay, and you're not lazy."

Chris had tried to will his body to work since the shooting, and it rebelled every time. His body wasn't ready, at least not yet.

I added, "You need to listen to your body and rest. I assure you the rest will heal your body. So please don't rush the healing process. It will take time, but your body will heal."

My insurance scheduled physical therapists and a nurse to come by our place during the week. Home health care was essential to Chris' recovery. They assigned two nurses, Caroline and Elizabeth, and two physical therapists, Michelle and Melissa. The nurses visited Chris for a month and would stay longer depending on Chris' progress. They didn't see the need to stay beyond the assigned month after they noticed how well I did with Chris' care.

His home care therapists gave him daily exercises. However, in-person physical therapy would help transition him beyond a cane for support. I watched Chris walk daily with his cane from the bed to the couch and the bathroom. When he walked, I noticed his limp and slouch each time he lifted his left foot. His left leg had lost muscle and now looked thinner than his right leg.

I silently prayed, "Lord, when Chris goes to in-person therapy, please improve his ability to walk and help him lift his foot at the same time. Please take it all away so he can walk normal again."

Chris saw physical therapists at home until April, and he made significant progress within a month's time. The next phase was in-person physical therapy at Tidelands HealthPoint Center for Health and Fitness in Pawleys Island. Chris looked forward to it because he noticed his body was healing, and he was growing impatient with the length of the healing process. Patience was not Chris' strongest virtue and my children have told me that it's not mine either.

But as the old saying goes, "When that's all you have, then that's all you can do."

The first day of physical therapy at Tidelands felt like Chris' first day of kindergarten. I was nervous and excited at the same time. I think I was more excited than Chris, even though he didn't show his emotions. Chris always appeared to have his emotions under control while the rest of us were on pins and needles. He maintained a calm demeanor the entire ride to his appointment.

When we arrived at HealthPoint, the facility had a strong smell of chlorine from the pool. It was my first time there, but I liked what I saw. I observed patients on exercise equipment in the gym and heard them in the swimming pool. I felt relief as it appeared Chris would be in excellent hands. I believed this was the perfect next step in my son's healing journey.

The receptionist gave me patient forms to fill out after she confirmed Chris had an appointment. He couldn't complete and sign the forms because he was still too weak to write, so I filled them out for him. One question on the form caught my attention and I couldn't wait to hear Chris' answer.

I asked him, "What do you want from therapy?"

Chris replied, "I want to walk better and play basketball again."

I smiled and thought that was a good answer. I knew Chris would mention basketball since it's what he loved, and walking was also important to him. I returned the forms to the receptionist and noticed Chris still looked frail. I was confident physical therapy would help him gain strength in his legs because he needed it. He still didn't have the strength to walk more than a few feet before he got tired and couldn't walk anymore.

They assigned Chris two physical therapists. I remember one of the therapist's names at the facility was Danielle. Danielle was Chris' primary therapist and made him feel at ease. Danielle worked well with Chris and showed him multiple ways to gain strength in his legs and entire body. Most importantly, she was patient with him.

I watched Chris struggle with basic exercises, as was to be

expected after all he had been through. Chris still couldn't perform the simplest of movements with his left foot. Danielle had him try to move his foot onto an item, and it was a tremendous struggle. I watched him attempt to will his foot to move with his mind, but there was limited movement. Danielle patiently showed him how to maneuver his foot onto the items she placed before him. I recorded his therapy sessions so that later, he could see how far he had come from a frail being to a vigorous man who walked straight without a cane.

The key thing was for Chris not to get frustrated and give up. My son needed to remain motivated so that he would continue his therapy. Therapist Danielle made him walk on something that looked like a step stool to strengthen his left foot and leg. I could see the frustration on Chris' face with every exercise. However, he did each one to the best of his ability, and that was all Danielle needed. I trusted she knew what exercises were best for his first day of therapy. The session's primary focus remained on his left leg, the weakest part of his body.

Chris made consistent progress with his physical therapy each week and didn't experience any setbacks. I watched his confidence grow as he noticed his body transition and become stronger. When Chris was alone, he worked on the strength exercises Danielle assigned to him. Chris gradually walked upright with no slouch while using his cane. He still lifted his left foot as he walked, but his posture no longer resembled that of a disabled person. The physical therapy made Chris' care easier, which allowed me to return to grad school.

Prior to Chris' physical therapy, he only left the house for doctor appointments and therapy sessions. So, you can imagine my excitement when he asked to go for a haircut. It had been several months since Chris' last haircut, and he was overdue. I contacted our cousin Jason, who gave my sons their first haircuts and was their barber for many years. Cousin Jason always made them laugh and gave sound advice in a lighthearted way, no matter the subject. Jason was well-known and contributed a lot to the Georgetown community.

Although he was happy to see us, I saw the look of concern on Jason's face when we walked in. He was aware of the shooting but hadn't seen Chris since it happened. After a brief wait, Jason motioned for Chris to sit in his barber chair. Chris got up slowly and walked to the chair using his cane. Jason couldn't hide the hurt on his face as he watched Chris walk. He helped Chris settle in the chair, placed the barber cape over him, and cut Chris' hair.

When Jason cut his hair, Chris' scalp was as white as baby powder. His extremely dry scalp was another traumatic reminder that made me feel numb beyond my control. Chris didn't show any reaction to his scalp because he knew my cousin would take care of him.

I explained to Jason, "When Chris was in the hospital, we couldn't moisturize his hair since he was on a ventilator, and it was difficult to move around the device."

Jason replied, "I understand, and you don't need to explain anything. I have to cut off all his dead hair from the trauma."

Chris looked good as new when Jason finished his haircut.

Jason then told Chris, "Your haircuts are free for the next year."

I was shocked and said, "You don't need to do that."

Jason looked at me and replied, "It's not up to you. It's up to me because it is something I want to do for you and Chris."

My cousin's response put me in my place. He was quite serious and looked like he would fuss more if I continued to decline his help.

I said, "Thank you, Jason. That means a lot to us."

I gave him a tight hug of appreciation before we left his

shop. My cousin didn't need to offer his barber services for free, but he wanted to, and it meant the world to me in that season. I was very grateful to Jason and his wife, Tynisa, who remained gracious and kind to us. Even now, when I see them, they both ask about Chris, and I tell them how well he's progressed. They always wish him and my family well.

In addition to Chris' progress, we celebrated other milestones in our household, like my daughter Bri's senior prom and graduation, with the help and support of family and friends. Time flew by fast, and Bri was such a tremendous help. She still cooked meals for Chris daily and ensured he ate before leaving for her after-school job. If I couldn't take Chris to therapy, Bri drove him and sat in on his sessions. She relayed the exercises assigned by his therapist and every detail of Chris' session.

We helped Bri prepare for a magical prom night. Anthony, Bri's godfather, bought her a corsage and made sure I took a picture since he couldn't be there. The pictures I took of Bri and Chris highlighted prom night for us. Bri was grateful her older brother was home to see her off to prom. Bri and I tried to keep our feelings in check, but giddiness overwhelmed us. It was both an emotional and beautiful moment as I watched them. I felt every emotion go through my body at once, but I didn't cry.

Chris stood in our living room and watched his little sister prepare for senior prom. He relished in the moment that he saw not only Avery go to prom but also his baby sister. He was grateful that he was not in the hospital missing this beautiful family moment.

Not long after Bri's prom, Money and I broke up. Before Chris got shot, we were already holding on by a thread. At least, that's how I felt. The age difference had caught up with us, and we were growing in different directions. Once Chris came home from the hospital, my sole focus was on him and his recovery. Money and I became two passing ships in the night.

My life was unraveling, and I didn't have the capacity to nurse Chris, myself, and my relationship with Money back to health. So, I sat Money down and explained that I thought it was best we end things. He did not agree and wanted to work things out, but I insisted that this would be best. Finally, we decided that we would continue sharing the townhouse until I was able to find a place for me and the kids to live.

Eventually, the kids and I moved to Surfside Beach into a two-bedroom apartment. My job had transferred me from the Georgetown campus to Grand Strand. The new apartment was smaller than our previous townhome, but the living room was right in front of my bedroom. While Chris slept, I kept the living room TV on and the patio blinds open so that I had a view of the outside. Both helped to calm my nerves as I watched Chris to ensure he was OK until I fell asleep.

The changes kept coming. My leave from work was ending, and I had to return on May 1st. Chris' physical therapy helped him walk better around the house. Still, I felt anxious because it would be my first time away from him since his hospitalization in January. I had to prepare myself to return to work and be around people other than doctors and physical therapists. I knew my return to work would feel weird, but it would allow Chris to be more independent and manage certain things without me.

I felt like a young mother who had to leave Chris at daycare on my first day back at work. I checked on Chris periodically throughout the day, and Chris assured me he was fine. He no longer needed gauze applied to his wounds. All that remained were scars on his abdomen, right knee, and leg. Chris now emptied his colostomy bag and cleaned it out himself with baby wipes. Our new routine still required me to change his barrier and pouch weekly because Chris couldn't change them on his own. I continued to refurbish the used pouches until the new ones arrived in the mail.

Chris looked forward to therapy every week. He would nap after because it tired him out, and his body was still healing. After his nap, he sat on the sofa and rubbed his left foot and ankle while he looked through his cell phone or watched TV. Before therapy, Chris used a cane to walk around the house. As the therapy sessions continued, Chris only needed the cane for distance walks. He rarely complained about the muscle spasms that infrequently bothered him at night. However, he continued taking the over-the-counter medicine Dr. Crosby suggested he take before bed.

Chris began to venture out beyond his doctor appointments and monthly haircuts. Over the next month, Chris walked upright and only used his cane as support for long distances. For instance, his cane was necessary when we visited Walmart or anywhere else, requiring a long walk from the car. Chris adjusted to walking more and was careful not to tire himself out.

I recorded him and took pictures each time he walked for an extended period to document his progress. He rarely caught me. I became a pro at stealing pictures and videos of him. When he did catch me, Chris would give me a look like, "Mama, stop." I felt if I recorded these moments, I could show him over time how much he'd accomplished. So, I recorded his walks to the barbershop, doctor's office, Walmart, and other places.

One day, my best friend Stephanie called to tell me her Uncle Gregory had passed. Chris wanted to see Stephanie and the family after he heard the sad news. He chose not to attend the funeral because he didn't want to go out in public, and the family understood. Stephanie's uncle loved Chris like a blood nephew. When Jasmar and Chris played basketball, her Uncle Gregory often picked them up for practice and spoiled them with treats and snacks.

Stephanie's loved ones treated us like family. We visited with them, and they were so glad to see Chris and vice versa. I knew my friend wanted to cry, but she didn't.

Stephanie kept telling me, "Shawn, Chris looks good!"

Stephanie's mother and aunts sat with us, and Chris was happy to be there with them. We stayed for a while longer before heading back home. Stephanie and her aunts hugged Chris and watched us return to my car. We waved goodbye and drove home.

⁂

BRI'S FACE beamed with happiness as her last day of high school quickly approached. Her oldest brother was there to see her walk across the stage on June 1st. After Bri's graduation, I planned a family get-together at my mother's house. Even though our relationship had ended, I invited Money to attend. He remained a fixture in my children's lives, and I was equally proud of all three of them for graduating from high school.

The day of Bri's graduation came. Chris and Money sat with me in the school's gymnasium to watch Bri and her senior class walk across the stage. Avery couldn't attend the graduation because he was out to sea.

Chris still felt uncomfortable in public with his colostomy bag. I made sure I brought a small caregiver bag for Chris' needs while we were out. I placed a dab of mouthwash in his colostomy bag so he wouldn't worry about the smell while at the graduation.

Chris didn't eat before we left the house because he didn't want to get up during the ceremony to clean his bag in the bathroom. Graduation ceremonies have sizable crowds, and guests must stay in the room until it is over. Out of all of us, Chris was the proudest to see his sister graduate and didn't want anything ruining the moment. All in all, we managed to have a wonderful day celebrating Bri's accomplishment.

⌒⋀⌒2₀

ON THE AFTERNOON of July 20th, while Chris was at a therapy session, I received a video of him shooting hoops in the HealthPoint gym. I was ecstatic to see him do what he does best – play basketball!

In the video, he said, "I can't jump as high as I used to."

I thought, "What an accomplishment, and without his cane! Only God, only God!"

At the end of July, I received a bill from the Patient Financial Services Department at Palmetto Health. I was floored when I saw the balance of $616,691.03. It was truly an astronomical amount!

I started to worry and question, "**HOW AM I GOING TO PAY THIS BILL?**"

After I saw the amount, I called my mother.

My mother said, "Shawn, don't worry about the bill. God got this! Leave it in God's hands, and it will be taken care of. Don't worry about the bill. Continue to take care of Chris."

Then I heard another voice say, "Look at the bill again. This time carefully."

I looked at the bill and immediately thanked God for what I saw. Only God! When I looked at the bill again, I noticed that after my insurance paid a certain amount and other adjustments were applied, there was only a balance due of $647.82!

I thought, "Okay, that's not bad. I could figure out a way to pay that."

That total was much better than what I originally thought it was.

A couple of days later, I received two more bills for $460.39 and $4,858.88. I placed the bills on my table and didn't look at them again. Two weeks later, I received a Notice of Award from the South Carolina Crime Victim Services Division- Department of Crime Victim Compensation (DCVC). It was a payment of $647.82.

A few days after that blessing, I received another Notice of Award for $5,319.27. This amount paid the remaining balance for every hospital bill in full! I didn't have to pay anything! Look at God! I embraced the relief and profound calmness that came over me. My anxiety subsided as I looked over what could have been a lifetime of debt now paid in full. It appeared the entire hospital bill ordeal was over.

Physical therapy ended toward the end of August. Chris now walked upright with only a slight limp. The limp wasn't as profound as it was at the beginning of his therapy. You only noticed the limp if you studied Chris' walk. What a beautiful blessing it was to watch my son walk freely again!

Chris had an appointment with Dr. Watson on September 7th, and I had lots of questions I couldn't wait to ask. I also hoped for good news about his colostomy.

I wondered, "How much has his intestines healed since January? How long until the colostomy can be reversed? If not, how much longer would he have the colostomy?"

I took the day off from work and drove Chris to Columbia for his appointment. I brought my caregiver bag with me. I filled it with pouches, barriers, cooking spray, baby wipes, alcohol wipes, a small bottle of mouthwash, and a white washcloth. The supplies were in case I needed to empty his bag or change the barrier after Dr. Watson checked his stoma. The barrier wouldn't stick to his skin in high humidity, so I had to change the barrier more in the summer and fall. I always prepared myself for the unexpected when we attended doctor appointments or went anywhere.

After Chris' examination, we received the good news I waited months to hear.

Dr. Watson said, "Chris' colon is healed enough for the colostomy reversal. We just need to perform a few tests to ensure he's ready."

God answered my prayers, and I wanted to jump for joy! Thank you, Jesus! Thank you, Jesus! I felt pure joy and happiness because this was a step towards Chris feeling like himself again.

Dr. Watson added, "I'd like to be the one to perform the reversal since I did the original procedure."

Dr. Watson gave us information on scheduling the colonoscopy for Chris. His staff would set a date for the reversal after the test results came back.

Before we left, Dr. Watson said, "Chris, I'm so happy to see you walking with no support! I'll see you guys in a couple of months."

Dr. Watson was ecstatic as he and his nurses watched him walk down the hall in astonishment. They saw him come from near death, being wheeled into the office in a wheelchair, barely able to walk with a cane, and now walking on his own. We left the office feeling like the future was bright.

Chris asked, "Can we go to my job before we leave Columbia?"

He directed me how to get there, and I tried to record him discreetly as he walked into the store. Chris caught me and looked at me, annoyed.

Pretending to look at my phone, I said, "What? I was checking my text messages! It's so bright out here I had to hold my phone up to see what I was doing."

He looked at me with an expression like, "Sure you were."

I walked around Walmart, picking up a few items while

Chris talked to his manager and some of his colleagues who still worked there. Chris found me as I was checking out.

I asked, "Are you ready to leave so we can get back on the road to Pawleys Island?"

He nodded yes, and we headed out of the store.

We talked a bit on the way home before Chris dozed off to sleep. I was still on cloud nine, thinking about how far we had come on this journey. Chris was going to have his colostomy reversed. God is so good!

Chapter 12

The Last Surgery

After receiving the good news of Chris' colostomy reversal, they sent Chris to Waccamaw Medical Center for blood work. The nurse informed us Dr. Watson would schedule a surgery date based on the lab results. Until then, we were to continue with our daily routine. I was just thankful that each pre-op request brought my son closer to his total healing.

When I arrived home from work, I noticed Chris was lying in my bed on his side. Lately, he had been lying down more than usual, but it didn't alarm me. However, this day, he had the covers over his head and looked like he was in pain. He laid still as though if he moved, the pain would worsen. I didn't bother him because I knew he'd tell me if something was wrong. So, I went to lie down in the living room.

Just as I dozed off, Chris came into the living room and woke me up.

He said, "Mama, my stomach and butt really hurt. I feel like I need to go to the bathroom like normal, but I can't because of the stoma. And I can feel mucus coming out of my butt, which is nasty."

I jumped up and said, "Get dressed so we can drive to

Grand Strand Medical Center. I think something might be wrong internally, and I don't want us to take any chances."

I thought, "Here we go again!"

Fear and nervousness filled my heart whenever something wasn't right with Chris. He didn't look well to me, and I didn't want to second-guess what was going on with him. Chris was weak and barely ate any food because his stomach hurt so badly.

I questioned myself, "Will I always go through this with him? Will he get sick at the drop of a hat? Will this be a constant issue?"

I didn't have time to entertain all of these thoughts. I needed to get him to the hospital immediately. I pondered if there would ever be a calm moment in my care of him. It felt like his body was constantly fighting something new, which left me overwhelmed and frustrated.

Once he got dressed, I drove straight to the emergency room. We didn't wait long to be seen by the nurses. They asked Chris questions, checked his vitals, and more. The nurses found a gurney for him to lie on so he didn't have to sit in an uncomfortable chair. They also gave him a blanket, which was nice. Chris fell asleep while we waited, and I sat in a chair by his side in the hallway. He was in a lot of pain and exhausted by the time they wheeled him into a room to be seen by the doctor.

The emergency room physician, Dr. Bomar, walked in to speak with us.

He said, "Hi, Chris! What's going on with you?"

Chris replied, "I keep feeling the urge to go to the bathroom, and mucus keeps coming out of my behind."

Dr. Bomar read the information on Chris' chart and was concerned, especially since he had a colostomy.

Chris said, "I really gotta go to the bathroom."

He got up from the bed and walked into the bathroom.

Chris ejected mucus and a little blood onto the floor. He opened the door to show Dr. Bomar the mucus.

The doctor said, "You may have an infection."

He instructed the nurse to have blood drawn. The results came back, and Chris' bilirubin level confirmed he had colitis, a colon infection. Thankfully, all other levels appeared to be normal. Colitis was treatable, and I was grateful Chris didn't need to be admitted to the hospital.

It felt like going to hospitals has become our routine since the shooting. When anything went wrong with Chris' body, it was important that we saw a doctor. The simplest issue might affect him. It was a tremendous relief to learn colitis was treatable and would permanently go away with medication. At least, I hoped it wouldn't return because I had grown tired of hospitals.

The hospital staff were really nice to us, but I constantly needed to expect the unexpected. What new calamity would befall my son, and how would I deal with it? My nerves became more on edge with every thought, and I tried to handle it as best I could. I didn't want to show signs of breakdown around my children.

Dr. Bomar prescribed several antibiotics for the colitis before he discharged Chris. We had to follow up with Dr. Crosby or Dr. Watson, his primary physician, within five to seven days. I dropped Chris off at home and drove to Walgreens to pick up his prescriptions. I also grabbed some food because Chris was finally hungry and ready to eat. Chris ate and took his medicine after I returned home. Then, he fell asleep in my bed. I laid on the couch. This way, I could watch him from the living room.

Chris was still asleep when I woke up the next day. Now that he was receiving treatment for the infection, I knew he needed to catch up on his sleep. I made myself breakfast since I was the only one who woke up early on the weekends. The house was still quiet after my meal, so I worked on my twenty-page class project.

Grad school classes were intense, and I was continually on my laptop, with sometimes up to 40 research books spread around me. My library friends, Julia and Roberta, would assist me with ordering from various libraries throughout South Carolina. I enjoyed history and researching my topics.

Truthfully, research and writing assignments were a welcomed diversion from what was going on around me. I could escape into the historical content and be completely involved in what I read. Chris no longer required a lot, so his care became easier. My son had a good appetite but struggled to gain weight, which frustrated him.

I constantly told him, "Not gaining weight is a good thing. When you're older, you'll complain you need to lose the weight you gained. Focus on healing and not on your weight."

I would be concerned if he lost weight. But I didn't see any issue since he had a good appetite and no signs of nausea or vomiting.

ONE DAY IN NOVEMBER, Chris sat at the counter of our small kitchen while I fixed him dinner. He asked me questions about his time at Palmetto Health Hospital as I placed his plate in front of him. I answered every question and explained everything from the moment Darius called me to the conversation with the nurse. I told him about me and Money's drive to the hospital and our meetings with the liaison, Mr. Johnson, and the doctor. Then Chris shared what he remembered from the night he was shot. I had chills by the end of our conversation.

Chris said, "I was walking from the bus stop that night and saw a car drive towards me. The driver pulled out a gun and shot me. I didn't see the person or the make of the car because it was dark. I felt the bullet hit my right leg, and the force threw me to the ground. I couldn't walk. At that moment, something told me to take cover in the bushes. I didn't know if the person who fired was gonna come back and kill me. I heard the car stop, then drive off, and that's when I called Darius."

Earlier that week, Chris had bought a new phone. He had been saving to buy a new car, and he and Darius had begun searching for a new apartment in a better neighborhood.

Chris continued, "I called Darius and told him what happened, and he stayed on the phone until he and Kevin could get to me. Then, I felt my body go cold. Darius picked me up off the ground, and the guys drove me straight to the hospital. My stomach was hurting, but I didn't realize they shot me in my stomach and right leg. When we got to the emergency room, the last thing I remembered was someone asking my name and date of birth. Mama, I heard your voice telling me to fight for my life."

What Chris shared next gave me chills.

He explained, "I felt like I was never alone. Right after the shooting, I heard a voice tell me how to maneuver my way into the bushes, which kept me safe and hidden. God and Grandpa Bruce were both with me in the bushes and the hospital room. They even stayed in the room when visitors came. God and Grandpa Bruce never left me, mama."

I felt chills go through my body as I looked at my son. I was speechless for a moment as I tried to process everything he shared. His life was indeed a miracle.

Chris looked at me and said, "I don't talk about it because people will think I am crazy for saying Grandpa Bruce and God were with me."

I looked at him and replied, "No, they will know you are a believer."

He shook his head and continued to eat while I washed

dishes and cleaned the kitchen. I left him to eat in peace and walked to my room. The conversation left me shaken. However, I felt God's presence because I knew He was there for us.

God guided me through Chris' entire ordeal. I recalled blocking everything else out during that time. I focused only on what God wanted me to do in that scary situation, which could have gone either way. My son could have died that night or days after. However, it was literally God who guided us both through chilled me to my bones.

Our conversation never left my mind, even though we didn't talk about it anymore. I didn't ask him a lot of questions because Chris only remembered certain moments, not the whole situation. I filled in the gaps for him, but the conversation still left me speechless after all he shared.

Dr. Watson's office scheduled a preoperative exam for Chris on December 28th with a gastroenterologist, Dr. Cornnell. After the appointment, Chris surprised me and wanted to eat lunch inside a restaurant. Until this moment, Chris had refused to eat in public with his colostomy bag. He shared his feelings with me after we sat down.

Chris said, "Mama, I'm really looking forward to my surgery. I feel like I'm one step closer to feeling like myself again."

It felt great watching my son enjoy eating out. He was happy, and I was happy for him.

Dr. Cornnell's office scheduled the colonoscopy for January 23, 2018. They gave us medical instructions and a list of foods to eat and avoid two days prior to his procedure. I bought everything Chris wanted from the list and the SuPrep solution he was required to ingest the day before the colonoscopy.

The day before the colonoscopy, Chris had to be on a clear, liquid diet, and it was a long night for us both. I changed countless amounts of colostomy pouches. I couldn't remove or replace a pouch quick enough. A funny thing happened while I replaced one of his pouches. Chris was in my bathroom, and before I could replace the pouch, liquid stool squirted all over my bathroom floor and door. Chris was embarrassed and apologized for the mess I had to clean.

I said, "Don't apologize because you can't control your stoma's liquid stool."

Chris grew increasingly uncomfortable as the night progressed because he regularly relied on me to clean and remove pouches. Both of us lost sleep from the continual process. I quickly cleaned each pouch and snapped it back onto the barrier, provided there was only a small amount of stool. If he had a lot, I had a clean pouch ready to snap on the barrier, placed the dirty pouch in the hospital pan water, and waited until he needed my help. I kept multiple pouches soaked in denture cleaner tablets and cold water.

The time came for the colonoscopy, and we were still exhausted from the night before. Chris fell asleep while we waited for him to go in the back. As usual, I took a picture of him while he slept peacefully. It wasn't long before they called Chris for the procedure, and I took a seat in the waiting room until it was over.

Chris' anesthesia was powerful and turned him into a talker in the recovery room. It was like he had taken a truth serum, and I could ask him almost anything! I laughed as I listened to everything he shared with me and the nurse.

He said, "I want five children in the future, and if my first kid is a boy, I'm gonna name him Quincy."

The nurse and I both replied in unison, "Quincy!"

The nurse added, "If I ever see you again, remember what you said today."

Chris said, "I'll remember. Thank you for everything."

We both knew he wouldn't remember what he said because of the anesthesia, but he was hilarious. The doctor briefly stepped into the room.

He said, "Chris doesn't need another colonoscopy until he is 50."

That was good news to hear. I glanced over at Chris' discharge papers and found images of his colon, notes from Dr. Cornnell, and the final results of his test. Elation consumed me to read Chris could proceed with his colostomy reversal! That was the best news I had read in a while. It meant Chris was well enough for surgery.

I shared the results with Chris, and he was happier than me. What a major milestone and accomplishment. Only God had made this all possible.

Dr. Watson's office scheduled the reversal for March 8, 2018, which was two months away. I slowly prepared for Chris' surgery and shared the great news with our family. My employer required FMLA papers again since the procedure would require Chris to remain in the hospital for a week. I informed my supervisor I wanted to use my annual leave for the surgery.

In the meantime, life went on as normal for me and the kids. I continued my routine of caring for Chris, completing grad school assignments, and working full-time at the college. I functioned as best I could despite the many responsibilities.

Chris still worked on his leg strengthening exercises. He only left the house to get a haircut or to take the trash to the dumpster. Bri continued her culinary education through classes at the college, which allowed her to continue assisting me with Chris' care.

February came and went. Before we knew it, it was March 1st. It was now time for Chris' appointment with Dr. Watson.

So, we made the trip back to Columbia for the appointment, where Dr. Watson's staff gave us several instructions for Chris' pre-op diet.

Dr. Watson said, "I want to set your mind at ease. I really feel Chris' surgery should go well, and he will be in the hospital for only a week."

Chris wanted us to stop by his former job after the appointment to let them know about his upcoming surgery. His managers and supervisors all wished him well. After we arrived home, I made reservations at a hotel near the surgery hospital to check in on March 6th for his pre-op examination on March 7th.

Chris' 25th birthday was on March 3rd, and we prepared for his sixth and final surgery. I sat on my bed and reflected on how far we had come. My emotional reflection on this entire journey transformed into concern. This surgery was as serious as all the others. Even though Dr. Watson had performed dozens of colostomy reversals, I was still concerned.

Chris was optimistic his last surgery would go well because he was ready to use the bathroom like a normal person. Even though he grew accustomed to the colostomy, I knew he prayed it wasn't permanent. The procedure sounded so simple. Just connect the pipes. I knew it was more technical than that, but it helped me to apply simple logic to something so serious as this surgery.

I received approval for my FMLA a few days before Chris' procedure. This allowed me to focus on our week's stay in Columbia. I packed everything we needed, along with our clothes and colostomy supplies. Then, I paid Palmetto Health the pre-op deposit for Chris' surgery.

On the morning of March 6th, we made our way to Columbia. We checked into the hotel and settled in for the night so we'd be ready for Chris' pre-op appointment the next day. Chris' appointment lasted an hour while the nurse checked his vitals and bloodwork. After we left, I took Chris back to the hotel and drove to Walmart to purchase the items from the clear liquid diet list.

It would be another long night for us both. Chris would be hungry and irritable again because he couldn't have solid food. I also prepared the SuPrep solution and gave him an enema. Can you imagine that? Chris felt horrified. I had to do the enema, but I reminded him that I used to change his diapers when he was a baby. I understood his concern, but it had to be done. The look he gave me after I finished made me laugh.

Chris said, "I feel so violated!"

I replied, "I assure you it's ok."

It exhausted me after being up all night emptying and cleaning colostomy bags. We had to be at the hospital by 5:30 am, and they gave Chris anesthesia shortly after we arrived. I sat with him until they took him back for surgery. I believed it was going to be a good day and that my son's surgery would be successful. It was my Aunt Frances' birthday, which made it a double blessing.

I watched Chris close his eyes, and I took one more picture of him because he looked so peaceful. Finally, the nurse came in to take him to surgery. I kissed his forehead and closed my eyes while silently praying over him.

I said, "I love you, Chris!"

To my surprise, he sleepily replied, "I love you too, Mama."

I became teary-eyed from the happiness and fear that coexisted in my heart. As I watched Chris be wheeled away, I said another prayer for him.

I prayed, "Please God, guide Dr. Watson's hands once more, please. I need this surgery to be successful."

The surgery felt like it took all day. I didn't see Chris until after 4:00 pm. When they told me his surgery was successful, I released a relieved, "Thank you, Jesus! Thank you!"

Once I laid my eyes on Chris and saw him peacefully

sleeping, I took more pictures. I knew he would thank me later for the memories.

I sat with him for a couple more hours. Then, my energy faded. I needed rest because I was still exhausted from the previous night. So, I left the hospital and drove to the hotel. Once there, I took a much-needed shower. Then, fell asleep the moment my head hit the pillow. For once, I enjoyed a sound, relaxed sleep.

I awoke the next morning excited to see Chris and prepared for a full day at the hospital. I took my library books and laptop with me so I could work on my research paper. I was one class away from completing graduate school. This class prepared me to write my capstone, and I had a lot of work to do.

Each day, while Chris slept, I worked on my research paper and other assignments for my class. My advisor and instructor were fully aware of my situation. They said to email them if I needed more time to turn in my assignments. Thankfully, I had met every assignment deadline thus far.

Dr. Watson visited Chris two days after surgery. He opened Chris' hospital gown so I could view his work. Chris had staples on his stomach and the stoma site. I was in awe of how beautiful the line of staples looked. I imagined that once healed, it would be a perfectly thin-lined scar.

I said, "Thank you, Dr. Watson, for doing a good job on Chris."

I took a picture of the area as a reminder.

Chris looked at me and silently said with his face, "Really, Mama!"

I was happy to see how well his stomach looked. Chris went back to sleep after Dr. Watson's visit, and I returned to my class assignments.

Chris progressed so well in those five days and received good news. He could now eat solid food! He was ready to eat and ordered broccoli, green beans, and meatloaf as his first meal from the menu. Chris was in heaven after his food arrived. It had been almost a week since he had eaten actual food.

I watched him eat and remembered the noises he made as a toddler while eating. I thought I heard him making those same noises as he was eating, but it was my imagination. You could tell he savored each bite of his food as he ate and enjoyed every bit until he finished it all.

It was good that he enjoyed it because the next day, things went downhill.

Chapter 13

Déjà Vu

It wasn't long after Chris ate his first meal that he became ill. He couldn't hold any food down and vomited every day. He threw up throughout the day, and it sounded nasty. It wasn't regular vomit to me because it looked green. Chris lost weight, and his spirit spiraled. He had no control over the vomiting and wanted it to stop. He was tired of the hospital, tired of throwing up, tired of it all. He was just plain exhausted.

Chris' uncontrollable vomiting increased my concern and fear. He was supposed to eat regular food, so what was wrong now? What was the cause? This was not supposed to happen. I couldn't control Chris' body, and I anxiously needed to speak with the doctors about his condition. However, any negative news would be overwhelming.

I just prayed, "God, please fix Chris so we can go home."

Chris looked at me and said, "Mama, I can't do this anymore, and I want to go home."

The look on his face was a plea for help. It scared me because I had never seen this look before. It was sad, and his morale was very low. His condition was getting worse. I tried to hide my fear from him because Chris never gave up on anything.

I wondered, "What is taking the doctors so long to diagnose Chris? They need to fix this because he looks like he is dying."

Once again, I had no control over my son's situation. I helplessly watched him become sicker and sicker. I could only try to show optimism and assure him everything would be fine, even though I saw the complete opposite.

I told Chris, "The doctors won't let you go home in your current condition, and they will find the cause of your severe vomiting."

I thought the surgery was successful. So, what happened? Why was Chris not progressing? Why was my son so sick?

I sat in the chair and resolved to remain optimistic that the doctors would find the cause of his vomiting. But I became more frightened with each second and minute that passed without a diagnosis for my son. I watched him become morbidly skinnier and weaker. His body mass was below normal. He was so thin it scared me. I honestly felt I was watching a walking skeleton every time he trudged to the bathroom to vomit with his intravenous line.

Chris could barely lift his head, better yet, walk to the bathroom to throw up. His vomiting sounded painful. I conditioned myself to stay strong because I didn't want Chris to see me fall apart. I silently prayed every time he walked to the bathroom and back to his bed. He didn't know that I closed my eyes and rocked in my seat, praying for him to get better whenever I heard him vomit. I ended my prayers when I heard the bathroom door open and watched him walk back to bed.

Once he was back in bed, I got up, put the covers back over him, and sat down watching him until he fell asleep. He was too weak even to pull the covers over his thin body. Just as when he was in the hospital after being shot, I resumed watching him breathe because I was terrified that he would stop.

While he slept, I continuously prayed internally, "God, please don't let him stop breathing. Please heal him. Please! Keep the doctors from saying there is nothing they can do for my son."

⁓⁓2.

WE WERE STILL at Palmetto a week later, and Chris hadn't improved. In my head, I told myself this was not good, and I prayed to God for Chris not to die on me. My fear of the unexpected caused me to pray endlessly because I wasn't in control of anything. One of Chris' doctors came in and removed the staples from his stomach, which left a scar.

Chris didn't say whether or not it hurt because he was too weak. I watched my son deteriorate in front of my eyes, and I felt defeated. A one-week hospital stay turned into two and a half weeks. The doctors still tried to figure out what was going on with Chris.

This ordeal also prevented us from moving forward and attending important events. I missed the funeral of my former boss and mentor, Mr. Vernon. He became ill and passed away while we waited for Chris to be diagnosed. I felt so bad I couldn't attend his funeral, but Chris needed me.

On March 20th, Dr. Thomas scheduled an X-ray to find the cause of Chris' illness. I followed Chris to the lab and watched as the technician helped him onto the table. Chris was so feeble, he couldn't move and just laid there. I rubbed his head with my hand as we waited for the radiologist.

Dr. Thomas and Dr. Watson came into Chris' room to update us on the results of his x-ray.

Dr. Thomas said, "The x-ray revealed Chris has an

obstruction in his small intestines, which caused the vomiting. The obstruction has probably prevented Chris from gaining weight since the colostomy reversal."

When Chris had the colostomy bag in place, he processed his food slowly, but the obstruction didn't cause an issue. The issue started after the colostomy reversal when Chris' body attempted solid food digestion on its own.

Dr. Watson said, "We'll need to remove a small amount of scar tissue leftover from past surgeries. The obstruction may have been brought to the surface when Chris' colon was moved down during attachment. We need to insert a thin tube through it to unblock the small area in his small intestine. By doing this, the food will flow through, and the obstructed small area will loosen. If this doesn't work, Chris will need another major surgery."

I thought to myself, "Another major surgery? Chris didn't need any more surgeries! He had been through enough. My son already had more surgeries in one year than I had in my whole life. And I had three foot surgeries."

I was optimistic. I believed the procedure was routine, and once done, all would be well. We could finally go home, and Chris would fully recover. I had to give myself a pep talk because the blockage in his intestines was an enormous obstacle to Chris' road to recovery. I hoped we were at the finish line with this last surgery. However, I became more concerned as time passed.

The next day, I stayed in Chris' hospital room when they wheeled him into surgery. I watched TV and completed my classwork, which distracted me from worrying about him. Dr. Thomas walked into the room and interrupted my thoughts.

Dr. Thomas said, "There's been a complication. Unfortunately, during surgery, Chris vomited, and his lungs collapsed."

What? I was confused, and my facial expression showed it.

He continued, "Chris suffered acute respiratory failure."

Still processing, I asked, "What do you mean Chris had acute respiratory failure?"

Dr. Thomas explained again slowly, "During the procedure, Chris threw up subconsciously, and his lungs collapsed. He is in the ICU, and you need to gather his belongings and go upstairs to his new room."

The trauma unit, the same place we were when all this first happened, and now I had to go back there! The conversation left me dismayed and numb because I couldn't believe Chris was back in the same ICU again. I couldn't believe the words that came out of Dr. Thomas' mouth, telling me Chris' lungs had collapsed.

Dr. Thomas gave me details about Chris' condition, then left me in the room with my thoughts. I wanted to cry so badly, but I couldn't. I was all cried out at this point. All I had done was cry since this journey began.

My only thought was my poor son. He desired to live, walk out of the hospital, and experience a normal life. I felt so scared and alone because my family wasn't with me. No Avery, no Bri, just me dealing with the situation and news alone. Once again, I felt so helpless.

I closed my eyes and took in a deep breath. In disbelief, I looked around the room and then got up from the chair with all the energy left in me. I gathered both our belongings and walked down the hall to the elevator. I pressed the button to the floor for the trauma unit and stared at the elevator door as it closed. I couldn't believe we were back where we started. This didn't go as planned.

Once I stepped off the elevator, I noticed the same receptionist from last year. She remembered me and seemed genuinely surprised to see me.

She asked, "Hi Ms. Shawn, what are you doing here?"

I told her what happened to Chris. She looked at the list of patients on her desk, and to her surprise, she found Chris' name. She told me what room Chris was in and buzzed open the security doors. This time, Chris was in the second room on the left. Previously, he was in the last room down the hall. I hated that I knew so much about this area of the hospital.

As soon as I walked into his room, I became teary-eyed, and my heart sank into my stomach. My son was on a ventilator again! I helplessly watched the machine breathe for Chris. I placed his belongings in the extra chair and sat down by his bed. I tried to look him over, but the endless tears of devastation clouded my vision.

I sat with him for a few more hours, then eventually had to leave. The ICU didn't permit me to stay overnight in the hospital. So, I drove back to the hotel and extended my stay, unsure of how long Chris would be in ICU or how long I would need to stay.

I was too tired to call my mother and share the disappointing news. The call would need to wait until morning because I desperately needed to rest. This day was brutal and left me mentally and emotionally exhausted.

I took a shower, turned the TV off, laid in the bed, and cried. It was the first time I had had an ugly cry since the night I learned about Chris' shooting. I didn't know what the next day would bring. I only knew that I felt exhausted, defeated, and helpless again. I don't recall when I fell asleep, but I did know we were back at square one.

I felt like I hadn't slept when I woke up the next morning. I got dressed and called my mother and sister before leaving the room. Then, I jumped in the car. The drive back to the hospital gave me too much time with my thoughts. I repeatedly played the events from the day before over in my head.

I kept saying, "This was supposed to be a simple routine, so how did Chris end up back in the ICU?"

I took this setback personally. As I walked into my son's hospital room, I looked at the tubes on Chris' body. It felt like déjà vu. Falling back into my previous trauma unit routine, I listened as the ventilator breathed for Chris as I looked around the room. Then, I sat next to the bed and watched him sleep. My mind raced with the errands that I needed to run. However, being with Chris took precedence, so I stayed with him most of the day.

Despite still needing to work on my research paper and wash clothes, I stayed with my son until I was tired. Once I left the hospital, I stopped by the store for laundry detergent on my way to the hotel. With my clothes and quarters in hand, I proceeded downstairs to the hotel's laundry facility.

I threw my clothes in the washer and ran back to my room to retrieve my cell phone in case the hospital called. After I placed my clothes in the dryer, I returned to my room, ate dinner, and worked on my classwork until exhaustion set in. I stayed up long enough to finish my laundry, then prepared for bed and hopefully a better next day.

Throughout that week, I saw two familiar faces - Ms. Carol, who cleaned the hospital rooms, and one of the detectives from Chris' case. Ms. Carol walked into Chris' room, noticed the ventilator, and looked surprised to see us again. I explained why we were there and that I didn't know how long we would be in the ICU. The detective startled me when he walked into Chris' room to check on him. The news of Chris being in the ICU also shocked him.

He asked, "Weren't we here before? What happened this time?"

I explained, "Chris had a colostomy reversal but experienced complications after eating his first meal. They found an obstruction in his small intestines and attempted to remove it. Unfortunately, during the surgery, his lungs collapsed, and so here we are again."

They heavily sedated Chris, so he was unaware of any visitors in the room. It was good to see them both, but I wished it was under different circumstances.

I went to the cafeteria for dinner because I missed lunch

and was hungry. I walked back to Chris' room after dinner and noticed his bed vibrating, but he remained sedated.

I asked myself, "Why is his bed vibrating like a washing machine? Am I seeing things?"

There was also a model image of the bed and its coordinates on the side. Robert, the respiratory therapist, walked into Chris' room and introduced himself. He read my mind before I could ask about the bed.

Robert said, "The bed's vibration will help move Chris' lungs since he suffered acute respiratory failure."

Chris woke up as Robert explained his condition and bed movement. My son looked confused as he felt the tubes on his face. He looked around the unfamiliar room. Before I could say anything, Robert stepped in.

He explained, "Hi, Chris. My name is Robert, and I'm your respiratory therapist. Your lungs collapsed during your procedure, and I'm going to help you get out of the ICU. I've got some breathing techniques that will help you."

Robert gave Chris breathing treatments and deep breathing exercises and continued with bed vibration. He also gave Chris a suction tube to remove the drool from his mouth. He struggled to control his saliva with the tubes in his throat. The tubes prevented him from talking, so he motioned to me if he needed anything. Here we go again.

Four days later, Chris improved enough with the treatments and moved back to a regular hospital room. This time, Chris had a PICC (Peripherally Inserted Central Catheter) in his left arm. It was a long, thin tube that provided nutrients through his vein into his heart. His digestive system still couldn't digest food normally. The TPN (Total Parenteral Nutrition) helped him receive the nutrition his body needed. The TPN bag contained 2 to 3 liters of nutrients based on the patient's needs. Chris' TPN bag contained travasol, dextrose, nutrilipid, sterile water, calcium gluconate, magnesium sulfate, potassium acetate, potassium chloride, sodium acetate, sodium chloride, sodium phosphate, multi trace-t5 concentrate, and zinc chloride.

The combined ingredients smelled like ketchup to me. It had a distinct smell, but I didn't realize this until later when I administered the TPN bag at home. When I met with the dietitian, she assured me Chris' liquid meal was a good one, even though it smelled like ketchup. As long as it gave Chris the nutrients he needed, I didn't care what it smelled like.

Chris started feeling better and walked to the hospital sofa when he grew tired of the bed. His movement was a promising sign. I often walked into his room and found him asleep on the sofa. I sat in the chair and changed the TV channel while I worked on my class assignments. Chris' energy slowly returned, and he looked so much better. Even though he was naturally skinny, he no longer looked morbidly thin.

One day, the hospital chaplain came by Chris' room while he was sleeping.

She knocked on the door and asked, "May I come in?"

I replied, "Yes, of course."

We spoke for a while about our situation.

The Chaplain then asked, "Can I pray with you guys?"

I said, "Yes, I would appreciate that. Thank you so much."

She prayed for us and marveled at how peaceful Chris looked. I hadn't noticed until she pointed it out. I observed him, and Chris really seemed at peace despite the issues from this last surgery.

She asked, "Would it be OK if I came back to check on you guys again? Your story really touched me."

I said, "Yes, anytime. I would love it if you visited with us again."

We said our goodbyes and the chaplain left the room as quietly as she had entered. I needed every prayer at that moment, and it brought me comfort. I knew God's peace was with us because it was on my son's face.

The same chaplain returned a few days later while Chris was awake, and I introduced them.

I said, "Chris, this is the hospital chaplain who visited and prayed with us a few days ago."

Chris said, "Thank you for praying for us."

The chaplain asked, "Can I pray with you guys again? Let's join hands."

We all bowed our heads in unison as Chris and I listened to her pray.

When she finished, we all said, "Amen."

I shook her hand and said, "Thank you again. The prayer really encouraged and uplifted me."

The chaplain shook Chris' hand and prepared to leave.

She said, "Chris, I wish you a full recovery. God bless you both."

The chaplain quietly walked out of the room.

A day later, I met a reverend named Sara from Oak Grove Baptist Church in the elevator. I told her about Chris' journey.

She said, "My son is in a room down the hall from Chris. Is it ok if I visit your son?"

I replied, "Yes, anytime."

She walked in a little later and observed Chris in his bed.

Reverend Sara said, "He looks so peaceful. God has Chris in His hands."

I felt God sent these two women as a sign for me not to doubt His work. God was there with us the whole time, and He wouldn't forsake us. A calmness and comfort came over me. It lightened my soul, and I felt so much better. It was confirmation God heard every one of my prayers. Now, I just needed him to answer my prayers for Chris' healing and release from the hospital.

Chapter 14

Answered Prayers

The doctors gave us great news on the morning of March 29th. Chris was well enough to go home, and his discharge papers were being processed! However, my excitement dwindled as we waited hours for his release. The wait was so long Chris had enough time to order and eat lunch.

A nurse finally came into the room with Chris' discharge documents and additional supplies. Finally, we could leave the hospital after Chris finished lunch. They gave us more supplies for the TPN than when Chris had the colostomy. The reserve included alcohol wipes, gloves, batteries, empty syringes with needles, tubes, and more.

The hospital scheduled a nurse to visit the following day to show me how to change Chris' TPN bag. It was larger, about 2 to 3 liters, and very heavy. The TPN bag came with its own black backpack for Chris to carry on his back. Chris would use the hospital's TPN bag until additional bags arrived.

It was imperative that I learn how to change the bag properly. I had to change it every 24 hours at the same time. The bag came with a battery-operated Curlin pump. The batteries and the bag also had to be changed every 24 hours. The pump operated all day and night to push nutrients through my son's veins.

The new daily routine scared me. The TPN bag process came with additional steps. Also, the bags had to be refrigerated. I stored them in my refrigerator crisper drawer once we arrived home. The vial of vitamins had to be stored in the refrigerator as well. I kept the extra supplies in our living room because it was more accessible for bag changes.

The home care nurse arrived the next day. Since 24 hours had passed, the bag needed to be changed. She showed me step-by-step how to change the TPN bag properly. Honestly, there were so many steps that I felt overwhelmed and didn't believe I could do it.

I wondered, "Why can't she come to our apartment every day and change his TPN bag?"

The home care nurse showed me once. Then, I had to replicate her and change the TPN bag on my own. She encouraged me with each step, but I still felt overwhelmed and frustrated. I used the laminated guide of instructions next to my supplies. The laminated guide helped more than she did.

The nurse said, "You should lay your laminated instructions on the table and place the supplies on top of it for tomorrow because it will save you time. Don't worry. You'll get used to the process. It will get easier and become part of your routine."

The first time I administered the TPN by myself took a little longer than I hoped. But she was right. It became second nature to me as I replaced the bag each day. I decreased my process time from 30 minutes to approximately 10 from when I first began.

I prepared myself mentally and emotionally to change Chris' bag from memory each day. It was not an easy routine to maintain, but I had it organized in my living room. Chris depended on me to manage the process because it was detrimental to his health and well-being. It stressed and intimidated me, but it had to be done.

I went over the steps in my mind with each bag change:

1. Sanitize my laminated guide before I place my supplies on it because the work area must be clean.
2. In the guide, there are four steps, and each step requires an alcohol wipe, two syringes of saline solution, and a heparin flush syringe.
3. Place two new "C" batteries near the guide, along with an IV tube, vinyl gloves, an injection cap, and a couple more alcohol wipes to sanitize the vials and caps.
4. Place a TPN bag nearby on my counter with two vials of multivitamins.
5. Wash my hands and put on gloves.
6. Press "pause" and turn off the pump. Remove the old batteries.
7. Clamp the tubing so it won't continue to run through the IV tube, and disconnect it from the catheter injection cap (green).
8. Remove the tubing from the pump door.
9. Clean the cap on Chris' IV line with an alcohol wipe and change it to a different PICC line. Whatever I choose, I need to choose the complete opposite the next time I change it.
10. Prepare to insert the multivitamin in the TPN bag; wipe the vial with an alcohol wipe; insert the syringe in the vial and push air in the vial upside down; insert the syringe straight into the TPN bag without puncturing the bag; throw away the syringe in the sharps container.
11. Setup tubing: remove the paper tape and throw it away; before hooking to the pump, spike the bag within the tubing, then spike the bag, take the cap

off the tubing, and insert the spike in the TPN bag with forceful twisting.
12. Hold up the bag until the solution goes through the blue air filter and flows through to the end of the cap.
13. Replace batteries and place the square blue tubing in a square hole in the right end of the pump door; place yellow flow-stop; close the pump door and latch it.

The steps were simple for a medical person but too technical for me. I also had to remember the clear and blue filters and the specific days they needed to be changed. On Tuesdays and Thursdays, I used the clear filter. On the remaining days, I used the blue filters. During this process, like the colostomy bag, I learned these key things:

1. Wash your hands.
2. Sanitize, sanitize, sanitize!
3. Keep dressing over the catheter site clean and dry.
4. Don't miss any steps!

I knew Chris didn't want to continue to take sponge baths, but we were unsure how long he would have the TPN. Chris hadn't taken a shower in a month because of his hospital stay. Then, I had an "aha" moment! I figured I could cover his PICC line so he could wash his skinny body. I believed he would feel better about himself if he took a shower.

So, I looked at his line, unclamped his tubing, and paused his pump. I placed plastic wrap around his catheter site and taped it securely so the water wouldn't seep through it. I had to be careful because I didn't want water to seep through the plastic wrap and tape, causing the site to get infected. I inspected my handiwork and encouraged Chris to take a quick shower. I didn't want water to seep through the plastic wrap and tape.

Chris grabbed everything he needed and headed to the bathroom. I could tell he was happy to have warm water and soap on his body and not just a sponge bath. He was in the bathroom for a good little while, and when he finally came out, he looked better. The smile on Chris' face told me he enjoyed the shower. My heart rejoiced at seeing my son appreciate such a small thing.

I never ran out of supplies and TPN bags because they shipped them directly to my apartment. An enormous box would appear on my doorstep, and right away, I knew what it was. I placed the bags in the crisper drawer as soon as they arrived. We couldn't afford for the bags to spoil. If they became compromised, I immediately informed the company to request a replacement shipment.

Chris hated the TPN bag because it was too heavy to carry on his back. He limited his walks to the bathroom, kitchen, and my sofa. Sometimes, he sat on the patio for fresh air but wouldn't go further. I felt Chris only moved in a triangle fashion in the apartment. He refused to go anywhere in public with the TPN bag, even though it was in a black backpack. No one noticed the TPN bag until they saw his IV tube.

Chris' nurse stopped by weekly to check his vitals and report to his doctor.

She said, "I notice your bag change process has improved. You're doing great! Also, Chris is ready to be taken off the TPN bag. His last day will be May 3rd."

That would be two days after my FMLA-scheduled return to work on May 1st. Chris would be normal again, and that was great news! No colostomy bags, no TPN bags, no more bags!

Chris asked the nurse, "Does that mean I can finally eat regular food?"

She replied, "Yes, you can have whatever you want."

I was so excited. I posted the news on social media. I wanted everyone to know how I felt about this wonderful news.

I wrote, *"Sixteen months!!!!!!! In a matter of days, my son will NOT have a bag attached to his body!!!!!! What does this mean? Well, as his mother, this has been a hell of a journey!! Emotional, overwhelming, and heartbreaking journey! Last January, a faceless coward shot my son eight times as he was walking home from work! This person did not know Christopher, nor did he know he had loving parents, siblings, aunts, uncles, cousins, and friends! This person did not know he was working hard towards his goals in life! This person shot my son eight times and left him on the streets of Columbia!!!*

"Imagine getting the phone call that your son was shot. While en route to Columbia, not knowing his prognosis until you arrive at the hospital? Imagine seeing your son connected to every tube possible, and as you look at him, his eyes and head swollen from all the blood transfusions and platelets given to him, you wonder what monster did this to your kid.

"As I set my eyes on him, I'm praying to God he will survive his injuries after being told he may not survive at all. If he does survive during the night, the first 24-48 hours are crucial. Every other day, he had surgery to repair his intestines, and each day, I witnessed him unconsciously fight for his life and God's mercy on him. I witnessed him heavily sedated and communicate to us in his way with a thumbs up, a hand stroke, and a nod to let us know he was fighting for his life!

"Seeing him talk and walk for the 1st time is a miracle, but above all, seeing him for life is beautiful! So, I celebrate sixteen months! My son struggled and persevered through his ordeal, saying very little, but his strength speaks volumes!

"A pastor and chaplain (both who do not know him personally) stopped by my son's hospital room and admired how at peace he looked, amazed he was not in pain, and told me God had Christopher in his hands! I know my son has a purpose! What is that purpose? Who knows but God? Only God!!!

"So yes, I am emotional, and yes, I am traumatized, but I am appre-

ciative and thankful for God's grace and mercy on Christopher and pray he continues to guide and protect him as he continues his journey through life."

I placed pictures of his colostomy and TPN bags next to the post. The images testified to Chris' survival and the painful journey back to a normal life. It may have sounded repetitive, but it was a written account of how this traumatic journey made me feel. We endured and could finally live a normal life. To know we no longer needed to drive to Columbia for doctor appointments or manage bag change schedules was an immense relief for both of us.

The home care nurse returned days later for the last time. I watched as she removed the PICC line and placed a band-aid on Chris' arm. The bandage was the only evidence the PICC was ever there.

I said, "Thank you so much for all you did and for teaching me how to care for my son's TPN bag."

She replied, "You're so welcome! I'm happy for you guys and wish you well."

As the weeks continued, the small round scar on Chris' arm was the only evidence and reminder of what he went through.

That Friday, I drove Chris to the barbershop. I watched as he walked in with nothing attached to his body for the first time in over a year! Oh my goodness, I felt so much pride as I watched him walk. Tears fell from my eyes because it was such a pivotal moment for us. Chris didn't notice my emotions while he walked so freely. This was a significant moment, a cherished and precious memory.

After Chris got his haircut, I bought him a regular meal to eat. This time, he held his food down without vomiting. Chris also ate all the food his sister Bri cooked for lunch and dinner without issue. He took the trash to the dumpster daily and did leg exercises to build his strength.

Chris still used his cane for support when he walked long

distances. He slowly regained his energy and strength, but it took an entire year for him to recover. We both knew Chris' body needed time to heal, so I didn't push him. Chris' short-term memory also improved from the prior year. I helped trigger his memory if he got stuck trying to recall a moment or ask a question. He constantly worked on himself. I regularly walked in the room while Chris performed leg and memory exercises. However, I gave him space because I knew he wanted to be alone to work on himself.

I requested disability for Chris while I cared for him because we didn't know the length of his recovery. Unfortunately, they repeatedly denied his disability application. Even though the Social Security Administration received proper documentation of Chris' disability, we received the following denial statement:

> *"Your condition resulted in some limitations in your ability to perform work-related activities. We have determined that your condition was not disabling on any date through 12/31/2017, when you were last insured for disability benefits. In deciding this, we studied your records, including the medical evidence and your statements, and considered your age, education, training, and work experience in determining how your condition affected your ability to work. We do not have sufficient vocational information to determine whether you could have performed any of your past relevant work prior to the date you were last insured for disability benefits. However, based on the evidence in file, we have determined that you could have adjusted to other work. If your condition gets worse and keeps you from working, write, call, or visit any Social Security office about filing another application."*

Chris' job at Walmart required him to stand and walk. Because of the numbness in his left foot, colostomy bag change, and deep vein thrombosis, there was no way he could perform his job. I questioned the Social Security office's review and grew frustrated with their denial. We became optimistic at the start of the new year as there were no setbacks and plenty of milestones. Thank God for that.

I recall speaking with my friend and tax preparer Brandi in January 2018 about the disability denial. She recommended a lawyer friend named Marvin. One day, while we were together, Brandi called Marvin and gave the phone to me. I told him about my son, what happened when I filed for disability and the two denials for his benefits.

Marvin said, "Ms. Shawn, I want you to call the law firm and schedule a consultation. I will let my colleagues know, and we will take your case."

I replied, "Thank you so much! I really appreciate it."

I felt relieved to know I would finally get help with Chris' disability benefits.

The law office scheduled an appointment in February. Chris and I met with Marvin's legal associates, Mark, Brynn, and Charlotte, with the Peper Law Firm in Charleston. The meeting went well. They asked me to forward all documentation and provide pictures by email. I felt the sooner I could provide everything, the sooner we would hear about his benefits. The lawyers also requested medical documents from each of Chris' hospital admissions.

The law firm worked on Chris' disability benefits case while we prepared for his colostomy reversal. I kept in touch with them throughout the surgery and informed them of his complications from the small intestine obstruction, treatments, and finally, Chris' discharge from the hospital. Our lives were returning to normal, and I anxiously looked forward to hearing from the attorneys. We had an appointment with the law firm a month after Chris' TPN bag removal.

We discovered the street Chris walked on the night of the shooting didn't have a camera. It was hard for me to accept they couldn't charge anyone for his assault. No camera meant no prosecution. The ballistic report concluded a 9mm gun may have been the weapon. Another reported shooting used the same gun, but there was no identified assailant. It all meant no prosecution or compensation for Chris' case. However, I was grateful Chris slowly continued to recover.

Months later, I received some news I never expected to hear. On Mother's Day, my youngest son, Avery, called.

He said, "Mama, guess what? I'm gonna be a father, and you're gonna be a grandmother!"

I replied, "Today is not April Fool's Day, so don't joke around."

He laughed and said, "Mama, it's true! My girlfriend, Jamaica, and I are expecting."

He texted me the ultrasound image. Oh my God, I was going to be a grandmother! I couldn't believe it. I was ecstatic. Their exciting news came at the right time. Our family had endured so much that a baby's arrival was the news our family needed. I looked forward to holding this precious baby and sharing the moment with all three of my kids. It was also a blessing to know Chris would be present to enjoy his niece or nephew. I thanked God for the privilege of being a grandmother. I knew right away I wanted to be called Nana!

Chapter 15

Surprise

I regularly checked on Avery and Jamaica after they shared the news that I would be a Nana. I was a hands-on mother, so extending my love and support from almost 3,000 miles away was hard. Avery and Jamaica had a gender reveal party in August. However, it was two days before I received my master's degree. I couldn't attend in person, so Jamaica's mother, Stacie, included me by phone so I could still witness the baby's gender reveal.

Once revealed, I was so happy to see it was a girl! A girl, my first grandbaby, would be a girl! I was so ecstatic about my first grandchild. I knew she would be beautiful and couldn't wait to meet her in a few months. Joy consumed my heart because I couldn't believe my baby boy would soon have his own baby. Wow!

Our cousin Toby called one day, and it was great to hear from him.

He said, "Hey! I would love to come over this weekend to see you and Chris."

I replied, "Sure, this weekend is fine. We'll be home."

When he arrived at our apartment, he told Chris, "Hey, I wanna take you shopping at the mall."

I said, "Thanks, Toby. I know Chris needs new clothes and is probably tired of always wearing the same clothes."

Toby watched as Chris walked to grab his shoes and walked back towards him. My cousin had an astonished look on his face. He was trying to comprehend how much his younger cousin had endured.

I smiled as I watched them walk towards the door. Their faces expressed a combination of pride, joy, and happiness. I was elated that Toby came to help and give his support. It meant a lot to me, but I knew it meant even more to Chris.

Hours later, Toby and Chris came back from the mall with a new wardrobe and sneakers for Chris.

Toby said, "Yeah, we had a 'cousin talk.' Sorry, but I can't share it with you. It's just between us men."

I didn't ask because it was their time to talk and catch up.

He added, "If you guys need anything, I'm here for you. I promise I'll stop by again soon to take Chris shopping again and check on you guys."

I hugged and thanked him before he left.

Chris was excited to show me his new wardrobe and sneakers.

He said, "Mama, Toby told me to get whatever I wanted."

I received more good news in August 2018. Despite all the obstacles set in my path, I graduated with a 3.6 grade point average! I was so proud of myself because there was a time when I wanted to give up on my education. My classes lasted ten weeks at a time, and they were intense. However, my education helped me through the most challenging time in my life. Grad school helped me channel my emotions into my classwork.

Weeks later, the college approached me about teaching an American History course during the fall semester. I was excited because it was different from my original goal when I began the graduate program.

My official transcript arrived from SNHU late, preventing

me from teaching in the fall semester. They assigned me to teach the Spring semester of January 2019. I always had a powerful love for history, and it felt right to teach it. The teaching delay gave me precious quiet time to relax after two years of constant projects and caring for Chris.

We received a copy of a letter addressed to Chris' lawyer from the Office of Hearings Operations. They requested all of his medical records and Chris' signature on an authorization release information form to expedite his claim. The sooner we permitted access, the sooner they could review his case and reach a decision without a hearing. It was good news for Chris and a relief for me.

I worried they would deny his disability application. Even if he received disability, he had lost wages from his work, and I felt they should compensate him. Chris didn't ask someone to shoot him and cause him to be out of work for over a year.

EVEN THOUGH I couldn't physically attend the gender reveal, I flew to San Diego for the baby shower at the end of September. I met Jamaica, and her parents Stacie and Victor for the first time, and they invited me to stay at their home. The last time I visited San Diego was four years prior when I attended the commission ceremony for Avery's stationed ship. I looked forward to sightseeing while there.

Jamaica's parents and I connected and became friends immediately. Stacie and I went sightseeing in San Diego. The one place I liked a lot was Coronado Beach and Hotel Del Coronado. Their beautiful beach, unlike Myrtle Beach, allowed a person to walk straight onto the beach without sand in their shoes.

We sat on the beach and got to know each other not just as

mothers but as friends. I spent most of my visit with Stacie and Victor. We discussed our kids, families, and careers. They made me feel at home.

I didn't want to leave San Diego because I was having such a good time. Avery took me to the Air and Space Museum, Balboa Park, and Seaport Village. I was so relaxed being out there, and it was much needed. So much had happened in a year. My spirit craved a change of scenery and, above all, relaxation. San Diego blessed me with both, and the weather was beautiful.

My daughter Bri planned our family's trip to San Diego. The baby was due the first week in December, which gave us an idea of when to arrive. We figured if she was born the day we flew into San Diego, we would be there for her birth. If not, then we would still arrive within a week or two after her birth. It would also be the first time all of us would be together since Christmas three years prior.

Most babies are not born on their actual due date. Well, at least I thought they weren't. My little granddaughter was born on her actual due date. I cried after I read Avery's text announcing her birth. He sent us a picture of her as soon as he was able. She was the most precious baby I had ever seen. Stacie also sent pictures of my granddaughter, and I fell in love.

I now understood how my parents felt when we had our kids. There was no greater love than being a grandparent because it differed entirely from parenthood. I beamed with pride as I shared the pictures with my mother, sister, and other family members. I was the first sibling to have a grandchild. We were all happy to have a new addition to our family after all that happened. It was definitely a joyous occasion for all of us.

I couldn't wait to meet my little granddaughter. I became more anxious the closer we got to our travel date. I was also excited for Chris, Bri, and me to fly to San Diego to spend Christmas with Avery, Jamaica, and her family.

Stacie and Victor extended their welcome again and invited my family to stay at their home. Stacie and Victor were flying into Philadelphia with their oldest son and daughter-in-law. They planned to meet their other granddaughter, Zoe, who was born in August.

I felt we couldn't make it to San Diego fast enough. Avery picked us up from the airport and drove us to Stacie and Victor's home. We all sat and talked in the living room. Stacie walked over and placed my granddaughter, Shanai, in my arms. She was such a little cutie pie, and I felt so much love for her.

The first thing I did was inhale her "new baby" scent. I kissed her cheek and smiled as she slept in my arms. Then I gave her to Bri, who held her for a while. However, Chris wouldn't hold her because she was so tiny. Instead, Chris sat beside Avery, and they talked about her for some time.

All three of my kids together at that moment was so surreal. I took plenty of pictures to mark the occasion. Even more special was when Chris held his niece in his arms for the first time. It took him a couple of days to feel comfortable enough to hold her. It meant everything to all of us for him to be there. It was amazing and precious to watch Chris interact with his niece.

I enjoyed our outing at Mission Beach, where Avery and Jamaica showed us Belmont Park and the beautiful houses along Mission Boulevard. On our way back, I walked behind the kids and delighted in the view and the feel of the ocean air against my face. I noticed Jamaica and my kids were engaged in fun, sibling conversations. When they weren't looking, I took a beautiful picture of them while they talked. Out of all the pictures I took of the kids over the years, that one was my favorite.

A few days later, we celebrated Avery and Bri's birthdays

because they were Christmas babies. Bri's birthday was Christmas Eve, so we visited Seaport Village and the Marina District. We walked around and took in the Christmas music and decorations.

As we made our way to the Marina District, we observed the USS San Diego Memorial and an enormous statue of a Navy sailor kissing a woman. There was also a replica of the end of World War II in 1945 and the USS Midway Museum. Everyone who walked past the statue took pictures with it since it overlooked the harbor.

We walked to the Port of San Diego and saw several beautiful buildings. We walked back to Seaport Village, and the kids took pictures together in the big chair. The boys took a beautiful picture with their little sister as she sat in the big chair, and they stood by her side like her bodyguards. They looked so grown up.

We drove back to the house to prepare for Christmas and Avery's birthday the next day. We walked a lot in San Diego, and Chris handled it very well. It was the most he'd walked since the shooting. Seeing he wasn't in pain or needed help was a relief.

Chris took everything in stride. He enjoyed the sightseeing as much as we did. I watched Chris to ensure he was alright because I knew he was still healing from his last surgery. Thankfully, his recovery was off to a good start.

We woke up on Christmas morning and exchanged gifts while my children prepared Christmas dinner. As I took in the priceless moment, I reflected on all that had happened. I was full of appreciation and gratitude that Chris was alive and there to celebrate Christmas with us. I knew it could have been so much worse, but I didn't want to dwell on that. I relished every second with my children and granddaughter. Happiness, joy, and excitement overcame me. I was truly a blessed and fortunate woman.

Since restaurants and other places in San Diego were

closed for Christmas, we couldn't eat out for Avery's birthday. We remained indoors and enjoyed the evening. Everyone took turns holding the baby as we discussed our plans for the day after Christmas.

Dewayne, Avery's father, scheduled a flight to San Diego for a couple of days. He planned to see our granddaughter and join us for dinner to celebrate Avery's birthday. Dewayne's plane arrived early in the morning, and he checked into his hotel. He drove to Stacie and Victor's house shortly after.

When he walked in, we were all sitting in the dining room. Avery handed our granddaughter to Dewayne, and he gushed and doted over Shanai. It reminded me of how he was when Avery was born. Everyone talked and took pictures together while we discussed dinner plans. Dewayne and I went to the store and purchased several baby items for our granddaughter before Avery's birthday dinner. Then, Dewayne dropped me off at the house and returned to the hotel to freshen up.

We arrived at the restaurant and ordered our food. I took pictures of everyone throughout the meal. We had an enjoyable evening, and the entire trip was nothing short of spectacular. I enjoyed my time with Avery and Jamaica. I cherished my time with my new granddaughter Shanai when I held her. I hadn't embraced an infant since my daughter Bri was born. I was out of practice with changing diapers and holding babies.

I loved every minute I spent in California. I took pictures of everyone holding Shanai, but my favorite was the picture of Shanai in Chris' arms. The image captured how proud he was to hold Shanai without dropping her. He also cherished the moment with her as an uncle. It was such a beautiful moment to witness.

Me, Chris, and Bri returned to Myrtle Beach on December 30th. Again, I had such a great time in San Diego. I didn't want to leave Avery, Jamaica, and Shanai. However, I was glad they would spend New Year's as a family.

Before I returned to work, I needed time to rest and be lazy. As we flew home, I looked forward to a better year with my family and my new role as a grandmother.

LIFE RESUMED BACK to normal after our trip. Chris continued to heal and recover, and Bri attended college. I began teaching history part-time while still working my full-time job. Both jobs kept me busy, and I was thankful for the distraction.

Teaching gave me an outlet for my emotions during Chris' recovery. I felt if I stayed busy, I wouldn't have to deal with my feelings from all that happened. Chris was recovering well, and that was all that mattered to me. I put my feelings aside like I always did and kept them hidden.

We received a letter from the law firm at the end of January. The court scheduled Chris' disability appeal hearing for May 30, 2019, in Charleston. The letter included a map with directions to the Appeals Office. Yes, finally! I took the whole day off because I was unsure how long we would stay in Charleston. However, I prayed the same prayer daily.

I prayed, "God, please let the hearing end in our favor."

We received a reminder letter two weeks prior. This hearing was the final decision, and I didn't want to miss it. Chris could receive compensation for the time he lost from his injuries and surgeries.

Chris and I met his lawyer in the U.S. Hearing and Appeals Office in Charleston on the day of the hearing. Our attorney, Ms. League, met with us while we waited to go before the judge. She felt optimistic that the hearing would go well and produce the needed outcome. We were called into the hearing room, and the judge asked Chris a series of questions. Then, he asked me questions since I had been his caregiver for two years. Afterward, our attorney gave an argument for Chris' case.

The judge replied, "You will receive a decision letter about Chris' case soon. I don't have an exact date, but you will receive a letter from the Appeals Office."

We walked out of the room with our lawyer toward the elevator.

Ms. League said, "I believe he's going to rule in Chris' favor. I promise to contact you guys with any news. Enjoy your summer!"

I was happy the judge heard Chris' case instead of just another rejection letter. I said another silent prayer in my heart and enjoyed my summer.

We celebrated our family's annual 4th of July get-together at my Aunt Frances and Uncle JB's house. Everyone was so excited to see Chris. It impressed our family with how well Chris looked and walked without pain or a cane. I received compliments on how well I cared for him.

A couple of days later, I recorded a live video where I contemplated talking about our ordeal. However, I couldn't bring myself to do it. It was still too fresh to speak publicly about all we went through. So, I didn't mention it again.

Chris walked into my room at the end of July with some unexpected news.

He said, "Mama, I'm ready to return to work."

I said, "Are you sure? I don't think you're ready to go back. You're still healing from your last surgery."

Chris replied, "I know, but I'm ready."

He had applied for a position at a resort in Myrtle Beach and got the job. Chris didn't tell me until he knew for sure he had the job.

He said, "Mama, I got the job. It's time I go back to work. I'm ready."

Reluctantly, I approved, and we worked out a car schedule

with Bri. She worked and took summer classes. So, we all used my car for transportation.

Chris' first day of work went well. He and I carpooled together. So, he dropped me off at work and then drove to his new job. I brought my lunch to work and didn't leave the campus unless I had a doctor's appointment.

THE LAST WEEK of August 2019, I received a call from my mother.

She said, "Your stepfather is in the hospital and isn't doing well. His condition has taken a turn for the worse."

I didn't like the tone of her voice. It sounded final. Unfortunately, Hurricane Dorian was headed toward the area. We notified hospice but kept my stepfather in the hospital until the hurricane passed because it was safer.

My stepfather passed away on September 8th, at home surrounded by my mother and all of his children and stepchildren. His former wives, Ms. Dorethea and Ms. Sharon, were also there to see him take his last breath. My soul was heavy as I informed my kids about his transition. I knew it would be hard for Chris.

When Willie was alive, Chris, along with my nephews William and Christian, spent a lot of time with him. They watched sports with their grandfather and helped my mother run errands. Chris would change the channel and help with whatever else Willie needed while he was with him. Chris didn't want to attend my stepfather's funeral.

Chris said, "I want to remember Grandpa Willie the way he was. I don't want to see him in a casket. I can't deal with that."

I understood and prepared to say a last goodbye to

another person in my life. I lost both my father and stepfather within five years, and the loss took a toll on me. Like Daddy's memorial, this was one of the hardest things I had to deal with. My stepfather had been a part of my life since I was 18. He was there when I had my children, got married, and moved into my house. He was supportive, just like Daddy. The loss left me numb and in shock. I couldn't believe this was happening again.

Chapter 16

Moving Forward

On October 9, 2019, Chris received an 11-page letter from the Office of Hearings Operations of the Social Security Administration. The judge ruled in Chris' favor to receive loss compensation from January 26, 2017, to August 1, 2018.

With careful consideration, the judge wrote,

"Overall, the medical evidence on record and the claimant's allegations are consistent. Thus, to account for the claimant's symptoms secondary to being shot, including abdominal pain, pain and nerve issues in his legs, and recovery from various surgeries, I find that during the period at issue, the claimant was only able to perform work at light exertional level, although he was only able to stand or walk for less than 2 hours during an 8-hour workday and sit for less than 6 hours during an 8-hour work day. I note that the claimant's limited ability to sit, stand, and walk would have precluded him from being able to perform work on a full-time basis. As for the opinion evidence, I accord little weight to the State Agency medical consultants' assessments that the claimant was able to perform work at the light exertional level with some additional non-exertional limitations. These assessments are inconsistent with the medical evidence of record showing the significant nature of the claimant's medical condition, symptoms, and prolonged recovery. Moreover, the consultants did not have the opportunity to review the evidence received at the hearing level, including more recent medical records, or to hear the testimony of the claimant and his mother. In sum, the claimant was disabled from the alleged onset date, January 26, 2017, through the end of the requested closed period, August 1, 2018, secondary to multiple gunshot wounds requiring significant surgical intervention and recovery."

Every time the consultants claimed Chris could work, he physically couldn't. They didn't give the proper analysis because they didn't have the resources to do so. So, they refused to pursue it further and continually refused to compensate him for lost wages. I hadn't planned to pursue the issue any further. I would figure out how to take care of Chris. I thought it was ridiculous to fight this hard for something Chris needed.

It wasn't until my friend Brandi told me not to give up. Even though it was a process, I was glad I didn't give up. I trusted Ms. League and the other attorneys to help us and, above all, placed it in God's hands! Chris won his case and received total compensation. The money would help him get his life back in order. They didn't give Chris a date to receive the funds. However, he knew to put it in the bank when it arrived.

Months after the judge's verdict, Chris came to me with an announcement.

He said, "Mama, I just talked with Darius, and I'm going to Columbia for the weekend. I think it's time for me to move back to Columbia."

Huh, why? Chris's words placed me in a state of shock. I

felt he was speaking in slow motion, and my eyes blinked slowly with every word.

My internal reply was, "Why go back? Why can't you stay here with me and Bri?"

His decision surprised me, and I realized Chris wouldn't stay with us regardless of the questions in my head. I wasn't upset about his decision to move. I simply didn't want him to move back to Columbia. He could go anywhere but Columbia.

My selfishness wanted him to stay with me. I wanted nothing else to happen to him. I believed Chris would be safe if I kept him with me and our family. I knew I couldn't keep my grown son home with me, and I reluctantly had to let him go.

I called Bri into my room so Chris could repeat what he said.

Chris said, "I just told Mama I'm ready to move back to Columbia, and I'm gonna meet up with Darius this weekend."

The look Bri gave him revealed she disapproved of his decision. Chris was ready to return to Columbia, and Bri and I understood, but we didn't want that for him. They shot him there, and he almost died. Neither Bri nor I thought Chris could drive himself, return for a weekend, or worse, move back there. However, my son was a grown man and had made his decision.

I said, "OK. If that's what you want to do, I understand."

Bri and I stayed on pins and needles from the moment Chris left until he arrived in Columbia. I worried if he was OK, even though I knew my son was with Darius and he would ensure Chris was alright.

Chris called us after he arrived safely in Columbia. I didn't hear from him again until he returned. Upon his return, Chris told us news we didn't want to hear.

He said, "I'm moving back to Columbia, and I've already given my two weeks' notice at work."

I internally screamed, "Why??? I don't want you to go back there!"

My anxiety and sadness soared to another level after I heard this news. Chris was fine, but I wasn't. I dreaded his return to Columbia because I didn't want him injured again. I feared I wouldn't have the strength to deal with another incident.

Truthfully, I knew this day would come, but I still struggled to prepare for it. Bri didn't respond. She just looked at him and attempted to process his words. Chris could tell we didn't like his decision, but he knew we couldn't stop him, either.

My son was 26 years old, and I couldn't make him stay home with his mother and sister. Living with us meant we knew he was at work or home and safe from harm. We didn't know if he would be safe in Columbia. We didn't want what happened to him to happen again.

Chris' news took a toll on both me and Bri's mental state. We internalized what happened to him and never went to therapy. None of us talked about what happened to Chris with each other. I spoke to colleagues, my mother, and friends about what happened, but my children wouldn't talk about it. It felt like it was taboo to mention it to them. I knew Avery and Bri didn't want to discuss their feelings unless they had to. Chris talked to me about it, but no one else.

It was hard to watch Chris pack his clothes the weeks before he left for Columbia. His room looked like a tornado hit it as he prepared to move. I didn't like his decision at all. Even though I knew he would be with Darius. I found it hard to watch him return to Columbia. I knew I had to deal with his decision, but I didn't know how to deal with it. I prayed for God to keep him safe because I couldn't go through him being hurt again.

Chris moved back to Columbia on December 30th. It hit me that we would ring in the new year without him. The day he left felt weird, like when Avery left for boot camp. I watched Chris place his clothes in the car. When he came back to the apartment for the last time, he hugged me.

He said, "I love you, mama. I promise I'll call you once I get there."

I smiled and watched him walk down the stairs to his car. I stood at the doorway and watched his car drive out of the apartment complex until I couldn't see him anymore. My eyes filled with tears because I felt a little lost, scared, and anxious. I worried about him but knew I had to let him go. I tried not to let anxiety get the best of me.

I prayed, "God, please bless Chris to arrive in Columbia safely and protect him."

Prayer was all I had. I also had to pray for myself because I needed the anxiety to go away. I prayed for a long time, and the more I prayed, the more I felt God's peace. I missed my son already, but I knew he would be fine. Once Chris arrived in Columbia, he did as he promised and called us using video chat. I could tell he was happy to be back.

He said, "Hey, mama, I made it. I still need to unpack and eat dinner with Darius. I'll call you later."

Bri and I felt so much better knowing that he made it there safely. It put our minds at ease to see his face.

I had to convince myself to accept this move. I looked forward to Chris' video calls during the week. I was glad to see his face when we talked. Chris didn't know I inspected him to see if he was alright every time we spoke.

I asked him, "Did you get a haircut?" or said, "Your beard looks nice."

Once I finished looking him over, I talked and laughed with him more. Every time we ended our call, I always told Chris I loved him. I always tell my children I love them because each moment I speak with my children is a cherished and precious moment.

The year 2020 came, and my children and I felt optimistic for a new year. I also looked forward to celebrating my 50th birthday in September. One day, Bri came to me, and we had a beautiful conversation.

She said, "Mama, I wanted to tell you I need to go to therapy. Since Chris moved back to Columbia, it's been causing my anxiety to escalate. So, I made an appointment at a local counseling center."

My daughter's decision to seek therapy also encouraged me to speak with a counselor. I was proud of her for making such a beautiful decision for her mental health.

I replied, "That's great, Bri! Would you mind sharing the counseling center's information with me so I can make an appointment for myself?"

I knew I wasn't doing well with Chris' move to Columbia. There were also other issues I dealt with that caused me to feel as though I had no control over my feelings or life.

The next day, I called to schedule an appointment with the counseling center. My first appointment was March 6th and my therapy session went well. Karen, my therapist, asked me several questions. I shared with her about myself, my life, and what happened to Chris.

I said, "I feel like I'm going crazy."

She replied, "You're not, even though it may feel that way."

Chris' entire experience overwhelmed and traumatized me. I felt I didn't have control of anything. We scheduled another session two weeks later, unaware the COVID pandemic would shut down everything! My therapy sessions continued through Zoom because it was necessary to remain indoors.

The entire world dealt with a pandemic that was out of control. Cases were being reported daily. It caused so many people to die or be hospitalized. We constantly saw body bags on TV being lifted into refrigerated trucks due to overcrowded morgues.

I continued my therapy online throughout the pandemic. I learned I wasn't crazy, but I suffered from depression. There are different depression disorders. Therapist Karen diagnosed me with situational depression.

My therapist explained situational depression as a short-term adjustment disorder. After a person deals with a traumatic experience, it makes it difficult for the person to adjust to everyday life following the traumatic event. Those experiences could be a shooting, illness, death, or breakup from a relationship.

So many things have happened to me in life, but the most traumatic was almost losing Chris to gun violence. I was constantly worried, anxious, and sad. I lacked enjoyment in everyday activities, like going to the movies and the mall. I no longer slept well and avoided social events and people. I even considered admitting myself into the hospital at one point because I felt unstable.

The feelings wouldn't go away. I felt worse every day. I felt no one could understand how I felt. So, I hid behind my smile and pretended to be fine. Deep down, I was far from ok. I hid the depression from my mother, children, friends, and family.

The news reported so much death that I refused to watch it. I didn't want to hear local, national, or online news reports about a young person killed by gun violence. It always took me back to Chris' shooting. I internalized the news too much. It caused me to think about the victim's family and how they had to cope with their loss and grief.

There were several times I would go into a trance after hearing about a recent shooting. It also impacted me if a family member knew someone who passed away from gun violence. My expression would go blank. There was an article online about a teenager who got shot while hanging out with his friends at a park, and he asked them to call his mother. I reached out to the teenager's mother because I had empathy and felt her loss.

I didn't lose my son to gun violence. However, getting a call from your child's friend about what happened is possibly the hardest call a person could ever receive. No parent wants that phone call or a knock on their door. It's what we dread the most and the worst feeling in the world. As a parent, you feel like someone pulled the rug from under you, and it leaves you with one thought, "I wish it had been me and not my child."

I had therapy every week throughout 2020. Therapy taught me certain things, like the news, events, places, and situations, that can trigger re-traumatization. Re-traumatization is a conscious or unconscious reminder of past trauma that results in a re-experiencing of the initial trauma event. Potential triggers are a situation, attitude, expression, or environment replicating the original trauma's dynamics (loss of power/control/safety).

My therapist mentioned I may have experienced re-traumatization based on certain things I told her that happened during my life. Every time I was told about a victim of gun violence, I felt I had no control over the situation. I felt helpless, hopeless, and overwhelmed, which led to anxiety. I would unknowingly blackout unless someone next to me witnessed it. I could still hear all around me. My mind would need to focus on something positive to draw my attention back to the present, pulling me out of my blackout.

I didn't believe it until a couple of incidents happened to me late in 2020. In one of my therapy sessions, I shared an incident that happened at work. A colleague was standing near me and noticed I was not moving. My coworker explained it looked like I was in a trance.

My therapist said, "Every time you deal with a stressful or overwhelming experience, your mind can't deal with it all at once. So, your mind will pick it apart to process it in pieces because it's too overwhelming for you."

I continued with my online therapy sessions and finally felt I had made progress within myself.

CHRIS WORKED and didn't plan to visit me until my 50th birthday on September 11th. Unbeknownst to me, Bri and Chris planned to surprise me for my birthday. This was the year my twin sister and I planned to celebrate our birthday together for the first time in years.

Unfortunately, we canceled our 50th birthday party. COVID restricted large celebrations with family and friends. We also didn't want to take the chance on any of our older family members and party attendees getting sick with COVID. However, Bri still planned a surprise visit from Chris.

Bri acted suspiciously the night before my birthday.

She said, "Mama, don't leave your room because I'm preparing for your birthday, and I don't want you to see anything."

My kids knew I went to bed early and didn't leave my room until I got up for breakfast the next morning. While in my room, I heard Bri in the middle of the night, making noise and moving things around. I eventually fell asleep despite the movement.

When I woke up the next day, my cell phone was flooded with texts from family and friends. I had so many texts. It seemed like everyone in my contacts wished me a happy birthday. I didn't leave my room until close to 10 am because I was on the phone with my childhood friend Kimaada.

I ended the call so I could get out of bed and make breakfast. I gasped when I opened my bedroom door! Bri knew I loved balloons and had filled the entire apartment hallway with balloons and 50th birthday banners. Bri covered our whole apartment with the number 50. I almost cried when I saw all the decorations. I knew my daughter put in a lot of time and effort to ensure I had a wonderful birthday despite the pandemic.

The day had only just begun. I didn't realize while I ate my breakfast and spoke with family and friends that Chris was on his way home. Chris drove two hours to celebrate my birthday with me. He and Bri texted each other to get me out of the apartment.

Bri said, "Mama, we need to go to the mailbox to get your gift. I got an alert that the package is in our mailbox instead of our doorstep. I need your help to place the gift in the car."

I didn't think twice about it, and we drove to the mailbox. The mailbox at the front of the apartment complex had larger boxes for packages too large to fit in the mailbox. We looked in the mailbox but didn't see a gift for me. Bri acted like she was upset the package wasn't there.

She said, "Sorry, mama, I misread the message. The gift is supposed to arrive later, not right now."

I replied, "It's ok, Bri. Don't worry about it."

So, we drove back to our apartment. Chris secretly parked on the other side of the apartment community so I wouldn't see his car. We proceeded to walk inside.

Bri said, "Mama, I hid your birthday gift in my closet."

I thought, "When did she find time to put a gift in my closet? I really must've slept hard and didn't hear her come into my room."

I had two closets in my bedroom, a mirrored one and a regular one, and I walked straight to the mirrored closet.

My daughter said, "Your gift is in the regular closet, not the mirrored one."

Bri turned on the light in the other closet. I opened the door and screamed! Chris stood in my closet with his arms folded and a smile on his face! I was so happy I cried and hugged him so tight. I couldn't believe he drove home to celebrate my 50th birthday with me.

He said, "Mama, I didn't mean to make you cry!"

I replied, "These are tears of happiness! I'm so happy!"

Spending my 50th birthday with my kids meant everything to me. I couldn't have the big party I wanted, but my kids ensured my birthday was wonderful. Even Avery, Jamaica, and my little granddaughter Shanai called me since they weren't able to fly from San Diego. Hearing my little granddaughter say, "Happy Birthday, Nana," was so special to me.

My mother and friends, Elanda and Deborah, stopped by individually so we could take COVID precautions. Family members continued to call and text me throughout the day. Elanda and I safely took pictures together. Deborah came by later and stayed to play games with us. We took fun pictures, but there was one picture of Chris and I together that I cherished.

We played one of Bri's card games. I went along with it because we were having fun as a family. It was my turn to draw from the deck of cards.

The card said, "You and the person on the right have to switch shirts or take a drink!"

We all laughed because Chris was to my right. Chris removed his white t-shirt, and I went to the bathroom to remove mine. I gave it to Bri, who handed it to my son. Chris wearing my birthday t-shirt that read, "Damn, I make 50 Look Good", with a silly grin was funny to all of us! You could tell he was a little uncomfortable, but I was happy he participated in the fun.

Throughout the night, we had a great time. My children gave me a memorable 50th birthday. What made it even more unforgettable was that Chris was with us to celebrate. Even with all that happened to him, our family felt so fortunate he was there with us to celebrate every milestone, family event, and celebration. Thank God for his grace because our journey would not have been possible without him.

Epilogue

Sometimes, anxiety gets the best of me as I still try to deal with all that happened. My therapist told me Chris' shooting will always be with me. I've found some ways of dealing with it as best I can. I avoid watching TV shows, movies, or news that include gun violence.

For instance, there is a particular reality crime show I will never watch again—detectives in the show search for an alleged murderer who killed a victim. The countdown clock ticks on the TV screen as the detectives speak with everyone who knows the victim. The detectives attempt to recreate the crime scene, find the killer, and solve the case within a short time. Most of the time, the show's victims are young African American men killed for various reasons. I physically became sick if I even heard the show on TV.

Gun violence was rapid in South Carolina, and it didn't help to know some of these incidents happened close to home. Even though I avoid watching media pertaining to gun violence, I am still aware of it because it appears on an app on my cell phone. Just knowing it happens close to home causes me anxiety and concern. It's a daily struggle for me, but I feel confident anxiety isn't getting the best of me.

Chris still lives a few hours away and has been busy working. He calls or texts me regularly because he knows I become anxious if I don't hear from him. He always has his cell phone in hand, so he responds right away when he sees my call or text. I do my best to hide my anxiety when I speak with him.

Since I'm constantly concerned about his legs and memory, I ask Chris specific questions about his day and health. Chris' legs bother him from time to time because of the weather, or standing or walking too much still causes discomfort in his legs. He continually strengthens his legs at the gym because his body is continuously healing. His work schedule occasionally prevents him from going to the gym. That's when he uses the physical therapy exercises he learned five years ago. So far, his legs have done very well, and I am proud of how he's maintaining them.

Chris' short-term memory will continue to concern me. It took some time for it to return after the trauma his body endured. Sometimes, I'm concerned his short-term memory may hinder him from working or living a normal life. His doctors gave him memory exercises and games to help him. I fear people may judge him because they don't understand him or know what happened to him. To clarify, Chris has no disability, and his memory is better. As his mother and caregiver, I become concerned watching him sometimes struggle to remember things.

I admire Chris because he's enjoying life on his terms. Every year on his birthday, he takes a commemorative picture to celebrate the blessing of still being alive. Last year, he flew to Arizona and watched his favorite team, the Phoenix Suns, play in the NBA Finals. Another year, Chris flew to Puerto Rico and sent me a picture of him enjoying the sun on the beach.

Chris also encourages and supports my decision to go to therapy.

He always says, "Mama, if you want to talk about your

experience with me, I'm here for you. I'm still learning and understanding all I went through, too."

I didn't want to put my worries on him, but I appreciated the gesture.

Earlier this year, I found the courage to talk about my son's shooting live on social media. Over the years, I spoke to family and friends about it, but never really publicly. I wanted to tell my son's story as I felt it may help anyone deal with traumatic events in their lives. It was also therapeutic for me to share my experience.

A month later, Chris texted me that he finally got the chance to watch my Facebook Live video. It made Chris emotional, and he was grateful for everything I did for him. He felt my pain as I described what happened to him and how it affected me. Chris felt the emotion in my voice and saw how teary-eyed I became as I explained every detail.

We talked about his time in the hospital in Columbia. He didn't realize how bad his situation was until he saw Avery and his neighbor cry. He was glad I emphasized positive energy, as it helped him subconsciously pull through it all.

Knowing and understanding how my son felt encouraged me. I didn't look for him to thank me, but I'm glad he admired my strength. However, I wasn't sure he would survive his injuries and surgeries. It wasn't until Chris' last surgery, the colostomy reversal, that he wanted to give up on his life. The procedure was tough on Chris' body, and he was tired of it all. However, he didn't give up because I told him to fight for his life. I was so thankful God gave Chris the strength to fight.

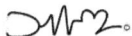

It wasn't until 2022 that I felt comfortable being in public or traveling since the COVID-19 pandemic. I took a year off from teaching and continued with therapy. I traveled a bit, ventured out more on my own, and started feeling more comfortable around people. I started going to events with my friends, and they were aware of my anxiety. My family, children, and friends became my support system.

One event I hold dear to my heart was when my friend Elanda invited me to a Gladys Knight concert in Myrtle Beach. I love Gladys Knight for so many reasons. Ironically, my mother's name is Gladys, and she is also one of my parents' favorite singers. My mother used to tell me how she and my father would dance to her songs back in the day. I grew up listening to Gladys Knight's music. So, when Elanda asked me if I wanted to go to her concert, I jumped at the opportunity.

The day came for me and Elanda to go to the Opry for Gladys Knight's concert, and I was excited. We stopped by Wendy's to eat and arrived at the Opry early to get a suitable parking space. We enjoyed our food until it was time to take our seats. We had great seats close to the stage. The music and lights started to change, which signaled the concert was about to begin.

Then, we saw Gladys being escorted onto the stage by a band member. She proceeded to sing her first song. The audience joined in and sang every song with her. Then she started to sing a song I was familiar with, and I almost cried when I heard it.

She sang, *"Smile, though your heart is aching..."*

I couldn't believe it! Oh, my God! Gladys Knight was singing my favorite song. I turned my head to look at the right screen in the auditorium. I didn't want Elanda to see my tears as I sang along with Gladys. The concert ended, but I didn't want to leave. I really enjoyed my first concert, and above all, I heard my favorite song. What were the odds of that happening?

It took a while to leave the Opry because of the heavy

traffic leaving the parking lot. Once we maneuvered out and onto the highway toward home, I still felt the essence of the concert. The concert touched my heart. It encouraged me to keep living, enjoy life, and cherish every moment.

People say my story is my testimony because they get chills when I share about Chris and all we went through. I get asked about Avery and Bri and their feelings, but I emphasize they don't talk about it with anyone.

After sharing our story, I typically get a startled look or widened eyes as the person tries to understand why I'm smiling. Once the person gets over the shock, they ask a lot of questions about my kids, mostly Chris and his well-being. I assured them that although Chris has been through a lot of obstacles, he's still here by God's grace.

People walk away admiring our strength. However, I want them to know no matter what they go through or how bad the situation is, God is always with them. I want them to understand that no matter the trial or tribulation, they will get through it. Every situation is temporary and will pass.

Chris decided in early spring not to renew his lease in Columbia. He came home and found a job.

He said, "I'm ready to move to Atlanta, Georgia, but I want to work a bit until I make a final decision."

I was just happy he was home. I enjoyed watching him be "Uncle Chris" to my grandchildren. I got used to him hanging out with his siblings and helping around the house. Each day ended with Chris watching ESPN or his cell phone in his hand. It was a daily routine until he came to me at the beginning of August.

Chris said, "Mama, I'm moving to Atlanta on August 31st, and I already gave my job notice."

At first, it felt like a repeat of his decision to move back to Columbia in 2019. However, this time was different because his father and his family lived in Atlanta. I felt confident that he would be fine. I didn't overthink his decision to move, which kept my anxiety calm.

During this time, I had the chance to return to the campus where I originally started working twenty-five years ago. It made me happy and excited to be with my campus family again. The transition back felt like home and like I had never left my colleagues.

Chris promised to stop by the campus to see everyone before he left for Atlanta. He surprised me one day when he walked into my office. When the door opened, I thought someone needed my help. I looked up, and it was Chris standing in front of me. I was so happy to see him.

I had a big smile on my face, and I shouted, "Chris!"

My colleagues came over and were excited to see him. They hadn't seen him since the shooting. Everyone was so amazed at how well he looked. After Chris chatted with my colleagues, I took him on a campus tour. He was so amazed at how much the campus had changed. After the tour, we returned to the office, and he said goodbye to everyone. Then, I walked him outside to his car.

He said, "I'm going to visit grandma before I leave town. I'll still be there when you get off work."

After work, I drove to my mother's home and sat with Chris on the porch. We talked for a while before I walked inside. Chris came in after some time as well.

He said, "I need to go back and finish packing because I'm leaving in the morning."

My mother immediately gave him food for the trip and placed it in a bag. Chris thanked my mother and hugged us both before he walked to the door. We followed him outside, and my mother sat in the garage while I walked to the end of the driveway. I watched Chris walk to his car. He waved before driving away, and I stood in the driveway until I couldn't see his car anymore.

I looked at my mother and said, "He's going to be ok!"

She replied, "He'll be fine."

I turned to look in the direction where Chris turned the corner, then walked into the house. I held back tears and said a prayer.

I prayed, "God, please continue to protect Chris and keep him safe."

I was so proud of my son and promised myself to always be there for him.

MY FAMILY ENDURED something we never expected to go through. I give God all the praise for giving us strength and guidance. Since then, every January 26th, I can't explain the anxiety and feelings I must overcome to function throughout the day. Believe me, I don't dwell on all that happened, but I still struggle with anxiety.

No one tells you unless you go to therapy, how gun violence affects your life and how to move on after the trauma. Some days are better than most. However, I remain astonished at how far we all have come. Rather than looking back, I am looking forward to more cherished moments with my children and grandchildren in the present and future.

About the Author

Shawn Wright was born and raised in Mount Vernon, New York. She is an adjunct history professor, a mother of three, and a fraternal twin.

As a teenager, Shawn and her twin sister, Dawn, moved to their mother's hometown of Georgetown, South Carolina. After graduating from high school, she obtained an associate degree from Johnson and Wales University in Rhode Island. Upon graduation, Shawn returned to Georgetown, SC, where she later pursued a bachelor's degree in library science, followed by a master's degree in history.

Shawn's life was significantly changed when her oldest son was severely injured in a drive-by shooting. Her journey with her son through his recovery and healing led her to share their story with the world. Shawn's desire is for their story to serve as a beacon of encouragement and hope for other families experiencing the trauma of gun violence.

Shawn finds immense pleasure in teaching all forms of

history and visiting historical places. During her downtime, she enjoys reading and spending time with her children, grandchildren, family, and friends. She currently resides in Myrtle Beach, South Carolina.

www.ingramcontent.com/pod-product-compliance
Lightning Source LLC
Chambersburg PA
CBHW070646160426
43194CB00009B/1596